THROUGH THE FIRE, BUT I DON'T SMELL LIKE SMOKE

By

ALICIA Y. BAILEY

Foreword by

Natolie Warren, Licensed Professional Counselor & Personal Development Strategist; Founder of The Whole Woman Experience

ISBN 978-0-578-48073-2

www.aliciaybailey.com

Instagram @aliciaybailey

PRINTED IN THE UNITED STATES OF AMERICA

Book design by around86-Fiverr

Cover design by germancreative-Fiverr

Edited by editornancy- Fiverr

To the loves of my life:

Jaylon, Jordan and Alia, my heartbeats, who are my reasons for living, I love you more than words can ever say and am proud to call you all mine.

Contents

Foreword by Natolie Warren

In 2004, I packed up all my belongings and moved to Atlanta to pursue my doctorate degree. I was settling into my new apartment, graduate school, my new church and my new life. However, I recognized that something was still missing as I had not found a hair stylist. After driving three hours back to Columbia, South Carolina, to get my relaxers for almost a year, I decided I needed to find a hair stylist in Atlanta. We as women can be particular about who does our hair, so I knew this may take some time. I eventually asked a classmate who was doing her hair and she referred me to Alicia. This was the beginning of me getting to know her and witnessing major events of her life unfold right before my eyes.

In this book, Alicia takes you on the journey of her life. With her, you celebrate some of her highest wins and you feel the intense emotions of some of her lowest points. What stands out the most is her unwavering faith, her love for others and her determination to keep going. Her courage to share her story with transparency, vulnerability and humor allows the reader

5

permission to do the same. She also challenges you to stretch in your own life as she encourages you to do your own introspective and reflective work.

From my perspective, we all have a story to tell that is filled with obstacles, challenges, lessons and triumphs. The beautiful truth is when we understand that our stories do not have meaning, we actually give them meaning. We have the power to give our stories meaning which determines our perspective of life. Where we are right now does not even remotely resemble what we have been through. The sequence of events in our lives, good or bad, happened in a timing that had to have been allowed by God. This is apparent in the specific people we have met in our lives and the timing of when we met them, as well as the opportunities that have come our way. As a Licensed Professional Counselor and a Life Coach, I know how our experiences and wounds can shape our lives. For some it brings out their inner strength and resilience while for others it causes deep despair and suffering. I can only imagine the silent tears, the unanswered prayers and the sleepless nights one may be enduring in their life. Although our lives may be undergoing a process that is beyond our current understanding, I hope we can remember that we are on the path to greatness so trust the process and keep going.

Over the 14 years I have known Alicia, I have witnessed her take those experiences as lessons. I have seen her have that inner conflict but eventually settle with the truth that was already within her. I have seen those moments where she did not know how things would work out and have watched them work out just the way they were intended to be. Unless she revealed her story, as she does in this book, you would never know what she has been through. She has gone through the fire and has come out without the lingering smell of smoke. Throughout the book, she demonstrates how one can do that and not allow their experiences to have a negative effect. By reading this book, you will gain greater awareness of how a bad situation does not indicate a bad life or the essence of your being. I can recall a difficult situation in my own life and how God reminded me that *your current situation does not determine who you are or who you will become.* This gave me the peace I needed, and I hope it does the same for you. Our circumstances are merely necessary parts of the chapters of life that are needed for growth and to equip us to handle much better the later chapters to come.

I am thoroughly delighted to recommend *Through the Fire But I Don't Smell Like Smoke* to everyone. Please allow the simplicity of this message and its power to bring hope to your life. Today you have the opportunity to continue to write your story and live your best life. I encourage you to do that and so much more.

Natolie Warren

Licensed Professional Counselor & Personal Development Strategist; Founder of The Whole Woman Experience

Introduction

What does it mean to be "through the fire but not smell like smoke"? It's my own interpretation of the adage, "When life throws you lemons, make lemonade."

I was born in Hampton, Virginia, to young parents who were still discovering themselves. I lived in a little white house right off Sherwood Avenue in Hampton until I was about 3 years old. I didn't grow up in the home with two parents who would live happily ever after. I believe there is some level of disfunction in every home, but mine was on another level.

I grew up in a place where there was domestic violence and emotional abuse. When my parents split, my mom had to work really hard to make ends meet and to put food on the table. I didn't grow up with a silver spoon in my mouth. Instead, I worked and fought hard for everything I got.

I suffered through being bullied and not feeling accepted. I had boyfriends who lied and cheated. I suffered at the hand of violence myself on many occasions. Life wasn't easy, but I made it.

I made it to become the woman God wanted me to become. I am still evolving into that woman of greatness through daily learning and experiences.

I continue to learn, grow and evolve into what I have been created to do. Even now, I must work earnestly to make things happen. On the outside looking in, people think things are just handed to me, but that is far from the truth.

I am not ashamed of what I have been through because all that I have been through has molded me into what I have become today.

Any change to any one of the experiences I had would have changed the outcome of who I am, so I am grateful for all that I have been through and for all the things I will go through in the future because the culmination of all of those things makes me who I am as a person.

Am I perfect? Most certainly not! Have I always done everything right? Most certainly I haven't! Will I make mistakes in the future? Probably! But guess what? I am me. I am who God created me to be. I know who I am and whose I am.

I am the little brown girl from Hampton, Virginia, who came from humble beginnings. I am so glad I don't look like what I have been through.

People look at me as a person who has it all together. I have my share of struggles, just like the next person. I get hurt and cry, just like the next person. But I choose how I will react and recover from those times of hurt too.

To share everything that I have gone through would take about three or more books. I just wanted to take some time to share some bits of my life to hopefully encourage and uplift you.

Even though you may have fallen, you can get back up. Even though things may not have gone your way in the past, you still can succeed.

I hope that while reading this book, you can hear and see my heart and know that the pain you may have gone through or may be going through won't last always. Remember, you can't have a testimony without a test, and surely, I have faced many tests and trials in my lifetime.

The great thing about it all is, I have been through the fire, but I don't smell like smoke! You too are an overcomer, and I believe that we all have a story or stories to share that can help one another. I hope that at least one of my stories will encourage you through your own journey to greatness.

I know my own journey to greatness has not been an easy one, but I will never regret what I have been through because I am able to help others through the process.

When going through, trust the process. It is really the attitude you have while going through that defines the outcome. We all are survivors of something. Know that no one has had a perfect life. It is virtually impossible.

Thank you for your support, and I hope you enjoy my story. God bless,
Alicia

What's Stopping You?

I've been a very determined person since I was very young. I've also been very self-sufficient and independent since I was very young. I recall my own mother telling me that she felt I didn't "need" her since the age of 2! I had to think long and hard about that statement. Why did she feel this way? And much less, how does a 2-year-old not "need" their mother?

She explained that I wouldn't let her do anything for me. She said that I didn't want her to dress me or even pick out my clothes, for that matter. She said that by the time I turned 3, I was already tying my own shoes, reciting entire plays including everyone else's part and reciting the Pledge of Allegiance too.

I thought to myself and even laughed to myself because I realized that I had always been a little ahead of my time and that I was always determined to do things my own way and on my own terms. I honestly can't explain why I was that way, I just was.

Telling me that I was incapable of doing something was not an option. If I set my mind to it, it was done. Once it was accomplished, I was on to the next. I excelled in school. Academics came very easy to me. I was the student who didn't have to study "hard" to do well because I remembered things well. When I read books, I remembered where the words were in the chapters and what pages they were on. Back then, I didn't know it, but I possessed a photographic memory of sorts. If I was paying attention and had thoroughly read the assignment, remembering was super easy.

At test time, I would close my eyes and actually see the words on the papers I had read, and most importantly, when I listened to the lectures, I could put myself back in the situation and remember the teacher's exact words. This was helpful and remains helpful even now.

Fast forward a few years. The determined, all-knowing, independent self reared its head again. By this time, I was in high school and somewhat of a typical teenager. I was definitely driven by that point.

My mother and I had not seen eye to eye for some time, and I was determined that nothing or no one would stop me from making my next moves in life. At 13 years old, I started working in a salon. From a very young age, I was fascinated with hair, fashion, clothing, travel and sharing with new people. I didn't know that part of me was being molded and shaped into the woman I am today.

Anyway, my mother and I couldn't get along. I found myself running away on a regular basis. At first, I asked my granny if I could stay with her. At the time, she was still an R.N. at

Hampton General Hospital, and I'm sure she thought I was a handful. My great-grandmother Moem was another place I'd go. Moem would let me stay for a few days, feed me and then by that time, my mom had figured out where I was, and I'd end up back home again. Another time, I went to my dad's house. Because my parents had split by the time I was 3, as a typical little girl, I always wanted my daddy and felt living with him had to be better.

That summer, when I was going on 14 years old, I went to live with my dad. Boy was I in for a rude awakening. That was a summer of hell in my opinion because the daddy I was so in love with became the daddy I hated. That summer, along with many more incidents, cultivated most of the mistrust and ill feelings I developed towards men that unfortunately seeped into my future interactions and ultimately into my relationships with men. We'll get to that part later.

Anyway, living with my father proved to be the worst decision I could have ever made. The saying "the grass is greener on the other side" proved to be an understatement in his household.

At the time, I was the oldest of 3 additional children that he had with my stepmother. My stepmother was a Caucasian woman, and if I had listened to all the stories from my mother, she was the worst person on the planet who had been instrumental in breaking my parents up. Well, you know where I'm going with this. I already didn't like her because I felt she had broken my parents apart. In addition to that, I had some form of prejudice and a little "black power" going on because I couldn't understand for the life of me how he had ended up with this white woman. What was his problem? The black woman wasn't good enough? So, I had issues that were much deeper than I knew.

Living there with them made me realize that even though I didn't necessarily agree with the things my mother did, her house wasn't as bad as his. Remember, I told you that I had started working in the salon when I was 13. The summer I went to stay with him, I was turning 14. I remember catching the bus to work or being occasionally dropped off for work and after I returned home, he would come up to me and tell me to give him my money. Had he lost his mind? What kind of pimp game was this because surely, I had missed the memo? So, let me get this straight. I go to the salon, work all day shampooing client's heads for $3 per person, and I'm supposed to hand my money over to you? I thought he must have bumped his head. Better yet, I did remember my grandmother telling me he had been hit by a car when he was younger, so surely that must have been the problem.

I know he didn't think for one minute that I was about to do that. At that point, I had to devise a plan. There was no way in the world I was going to do that. Who did he think he was? He even opened a bank account at Old Point National Bank that he claimed he was putting my money in and "saving." But guess what? I couldn't get the money out unless he signed the withdrawal slip too, and the crazy thing is, he could take my money without me being there because he didn't need me for MY money! I knew this picture was all wrong, so I figured out a plan.

Every day I came home from work, I gave him a percentage of what I made. If I made $65, he got $30; if I made $50, he got $20. That went on for the rest of the summer because he must have thought I was a fool or something to give him my money that I worked for. He was crazy, and I made up my mind even then that I would never find myself in that type of situation again with any man! Can you see where I'm going here? Can you say "daddy issues"?

Anyway, it didn't stop there. All of a sudden, if their babysitter fell through, my job was irrelevant, and I had to watch my sister and brothers. I had a very high work ethic even then, so not showing up for work at the last minute did not sit well with me. Surely, he couldn't be serious.

My siblings were young at the time, so I was in full "mommy mode" instead of big-sister mode. Don't get me wrong—I adored my siblings. I just didn't expect I would end up being their caregiver at the time. My stepmother and dad stayed gone. She was a pastor and my dad sold cars, so it was nothing for him to work a 12-14-hour day at times. I cooked, cleaned, washed and folded loads upon loads of clothes, gave baths, did hair, dressed and disciplined kids. When I say I cooked, I cooked. I was cutting up and frying two whole chickens at 13 years old. By the time I decided that I was going to move back to my mother's house, I had told my mother that I wanted my tubes tied when I reached 18 because I had decided that I didn't want any children by the end of that summer.

My mother and my dad's mother were so angry that I had come to that conclusion. What 14-year-old would be thinking in this manner? I was thinking it because I had had enough. I was only 14, but I had been pimped and used by my own father that summer, which was just the beginning of my underlying resentment towards him. My grandmother and mother chewed my stepmother and dad out, exclaiming that slavery days were over! There was the race card again. For a while, my grandmother didn't like my stepmother either, so this incident didn't make it any easier.

After going back home and regaining possession of my bank account, you would not believe how much money was in there. There was less than $200 in my account, and after handing him over my money at least 5 days per week for the whole summer, I definitely should have had more than that. I was livid! I'm so glad I had sense enough not to give him all my money. Do you know he had the audacity to go to my job to inquire about how much I should have been giving him? If that didn't ring "pimp" loud and strong, I'm not sure what did.

Determined to bounce back, I moved home. My dad was mad, of course, and at the time, I was singing in the Antioch Young Adult Choir. I absolutely loved to sing, and prior to me leaving his house, he punished me by saying I couldn't sing in the choir. When I went back home to my mother's house, I was under her rules and she said it was fine that I participate. One

Sunday, after returning home to my mother's, I was singing in the choir. My dad was at church and saw me up there and proceeded to demand that I come down out of the choir stand. Was he seriously trying to make a scene at church? So, this is where he felt like he could control two households. All I remember is coming down out of the stand and him being angry that I was up there. Some words were passed, and I remember him slapping me so hard that my face tingled, and I had a ringing in my ear. My Aunt Gloria, who happened to be there that day, immediately took me with her. I was losing my mind, and if I had been able, my dad would not have had another day to slap another female in his life. I had seen him lay his hands on both my mother and stepmother and I was plotting on him big time, because I hated him for that. Men who beat women are cowards in my book, because women are physically weaker by design. A 6' 4" man against a 4' 11" woman is no match, and that's how small my mother was against him. I can't remember how tall my stepmother was, but he still should not have put his hands on her. I was so enraged. I remember my aunt taking me to a small park in Newport News somewhere. She was trying to calm me down, but with everything so heightened, it took a while. She pulled out her Bible and started reading scriptures to me. Eventually, I calmed down, but I know I didn't engage with my father for months. It was a long while before I even spoke to my father again.

Strength, resilience and determination are just a few words to describe what was gained through this one summer in my life.

I often think about all that I have gone through and why I've gone through it, and the same conclusion is determined: to make me who I am today. All my life experiences, balled up together, make me the woman I am. It's up to me to see the good, even in the worst of my situations, and to be thankful for the lessons learned. I'm sure I'm not the first, nor will I be the last to have gone through it with my parents. I know I'm not the only one who has asked, "Why do I have these parents?" I had to realize they were used to get me here to fulfill my destiny. They did the best they knew how to do at the time. What didn't kill me made me stronger, and despite past situations, hurts, setbacks and unfortunate variables, nothing could stop me from accomplishing what I wanted to accomplish but me.

I believe that despite your circumstances and what trials you've been through, they are just a temporary setback for a big come-up in this lifetime. In the end, you can look back and say that all things are indeed possible if you only believe. There were lessons to learn from this situation. I could have continued to harbor hatred and resentment or choose to forgive. I chose to forgive in the end and to work on me through the situation. I had to let go and let God handle the situation. I'm sure to this day, my dad is not proud of some of the things he did, but from what I see, he is a changed man. Who knows why he did the things he did? I have been told that hurt people hurt other people. When someone hurts you, it's not your job to rack your brain to try and figure it out. Pray about it, leave it there and move on to set yourself free. Nothing can stop you from moving forward but you. We all have gone through something.

Moments of Reflection

What have I gone through that was intended to hold me back?

_____

_____

_____

What did you go through, and how has the incident made you unstoppable?

_____

_____

_____

Don't Touch Me!

I was 30 years old before I ever mummed a word about it. It was an ugly, dark place that I had tucked away deep, deep in my mind. I didn't want to face it, but sometimes, I was reminded, as much as I tried not to remember.

I guess there became a breaking point when the secret became so loud in my head that I had to let it out.

I remember riding in the car with my husband at the time. Mary J. Bilge was singing one of her heartfelt, soulful songs. To this day, I can't remember which one, but all I remember is I was looking out the window and suddenly, I just began to cry uncontrollably.

Of course, my husband was full of concern because just moments before, we had been talking and laughing.

I blurted out words no one wants to hear. "I was molested when I was younger." There! I had finally said it out loud to someone! It felt good to release yet scary at the same time. He looked at me with utter dismay, and I remember my first thoughts were, what does he think of me now? I was so innocent. I was just a little girl! "Don't touch me!"

For about 3 years, I was tortured against my will by my mother's best friend's son. Her friend used to babysit me quite often because my mother travelled for work. Oftentimes, my mom worked in Charlottesville and left me to stay there when she had to travel. Her friend had a total of four children: 3 girls and one boy. He was disgusting. He was a teenager at the time, but he was much older than me. Even now, I can remember the look in his bloodshot eyes. He was dark, lanky and had a yellowish tint to his slinky, devilish eyes. He smoked, and he drank Pepsi, and the smell of that combination appalled me. To this day, if I smell that combination, it grosses me out. I think that is one reason why I'm not a big fan of smoking.

He was disgusting. The way he would look at me whenever I arrived to her house scared me. I felt trapped. I hated going to her house. Sometimes, I wished I could disappear and run far, far away.

I used to wonder what I had done to deserve that type of treatment. I was too young to be sexy or seductive, so what was it? I blamed myself as if I had done something wrong. Actually, he would say mean things to me. In the grip of his arms, I would try to escape. He would grab me by my wrists and yank me into the storage closet attached to the back of the house. There he would hold me, so I couldn't escape, and he'd lick my face with his disgusting breath. He would shove his dirty fingers inside my private parts and laugh at me at the same time. I hated him. I despised the mere existence of him and everything about him, yet I could do absolutely nothing.

See, he had my mind all twisted up. At such a young age, I was forced to make adult decisions, and I didn't even realize I was doing so. He had convinced me that it was all my fault. He had manipulated me into thinking that if I had told my mother anything, I would be the sole cause of the breakup of their friendship. He convinced me that I would be the one to get in trouble for his actions. He told me that it would be my fault and that afterwards, my mother would have no one to help take care of me.

I struggled with that. I was forced to think as an adult would. It made sense. Where would I go? After all, my mom did have to go to work. No way should I have been contemplating whether or not someone would be mad or if my mother would be forced to find another babysitter. All I remember is feeling trapped. I felt closed in a dark place, both physically and mentally. What was I to do? What was I to say? He had convinced me that no one would believe me anyway. "No one will care about what you would have to say," he said.

He even told me that I would be the cause of our mothers not being friends anymore. That devastated me. I didn't want to be the cause of that. She seemed to really love her, and now that I'm a mother, I know she trusted her and cared for her as a friend because had she not, she would not have left me there in the first place.

Many moments I felt alone. I felt I could trust no one. My innocence was shattered, and I was forever changed in a way I could not describe. I felt dirty. I had become numb to it as if it were a way of life. It became routine. I would try to block it out when I went to her house, but it didn't work.

She was one of those mothers who didn't believe in kids sitting around the house in the summer. She would lock the screen door, so you couldn't get back in unless you needed water or a bathroom break. She was a big woman and a bit intimidating, so I was afraid to tell her. I couldn't tell her, and I couldn't tell my mother, so I suffered in silence. I used to try to go to an imaginary, happy place at times. Sometimes it worked, sometimes it didn't.

As time passed, I didn't have to go there anymore. In some ways, I felt free, but I was still trapped in my mind. There were some things that became constant reminders and would take me right back to that place, even when I wasn't thinking of it at the moment. There was a song called "Cutie Pie" and every time the song came on, I would turn it off. It was a great song back then, but it reminded me of a place of pain that I wanted to forget. The smell of cigarettes and cigarette breath mixed with Pepsi were reminders too. That combination in itself sounds disgusting as I speak it aloud. Finally, as an adult, from time to time I would see him near my grandmother's neighborhood. He was so black and lanky with those eyes— the eyes I would never forget. I'd see him, and he'd speak to me like we were friends, like we were cool. I would bite my lip and barely speak. Yet, like a rushing wave that comes crashing down around you, I would drown in bad thoughts all over again.

I was liberated the day I blurted it out to my husband. I was finally free because I had told someone. I had suppressed the feelings of guilt and shame for over 20 years, and it felt good to finally release them. It felt good to share them with someone because I had told no one.

Years after telling him, my mother's friend passed away. I still had not told my mother. It wasn't until she passed that I felt comfortable telling her and when I did, it crushed her. Of course, she asked me why I hadn't told her, and I explained to her what I just explained to you. I was in a very difficult place. Not knowing what the reaction would have been, I refrained from sharing as not to cause any further hurt. I had put my tough girl armor on and had tucked it away for so long that it had become a norm.

Hindsight made me ask myself, "What was the worst that could have happened?" I'll never know because the parties involved are no longer alive. And in some degree, that's when I really felt safe. I knew he couldn't hurt me anymore, but knowing he had gone on let me know he couldn't hurt anyone anymore.

Because I endured this situation, I found that it had affected me in ways I hadn't imagined. When I had my own children, I was somewhat over-protective. I would have killed someone if they had touched any of my children inappropriately. I taught them at a young age that no one was to touch their private parts and if they did, to tell me. My daughter was almost fourteen before I ever let her spend the night at someone else's house. I took my boys in the bathroom with me for years when we were out in public for fear that "Chester the Molester" was lurking around the corner somewhere.

I want to encourage you that if you are a victim of molestation or any inappropriate touching, you too can be healed. Being able to talk about what happened is a huge sign that you're on the road to healing and wholeness. I believe this happened to me so I could help others. At the time I didn't know it, but now I do. God is a healer, and you can be whole and unashamed because you have done nothing wrong. Talk to someone you trust and free your mind from the turmoil and destruction that can wreak havoc on your mental state and overall health. Be free and walk into your greatness. The things of the past are just that. Let them go! Move past those things! Bigger and better lies ahead, and you are not a victim but a victor!

MOMENTS OF REFLECTION

Has there been a time when you were hurt by something or someone? Release it here by writing down those things that hurt you in the past. Afterwards, be thankful, forgive yourself and move closer to your wholeness and greatness!

_____

_____

_____

_____

_____

_____

I Can't Believe He Hit Me

Summer of 1988 is when we met. It was my sixteenth birthday, and I was living with my aunt for the summer. Actually, she was an adopted aunt. My choir director knew I had a lot of turmoil at home with my mother, and he knew I would continue to run away if given the opportunity. He suggested to my mom and stepdad that they let me stay with her. I can honestly say that staying with her was the best thing I could have done. She understood me. There was no drama. She lived a simple life in Newport News, and I will never forget her positive influence on my life. She was an English teacher and a choir director. I loved being with her because I was grounded and felt at peace for the first time in my life. I didn't have to face resistance with her, especially when dealing with my spirituality. I was saved at a young age and although I didn't always do things right, I knew God. With her, I could be myself. When I knew I had encountered things of God, I wasn't judged or questioned, like my mother would often do.

I was in church at least four times per week when staying with her. We had church on Sunday, Bible study on Wednesday, choir rehearsal on Thursday and other functions sometimes on Friday or Saturday. I didn't mind being in church all the time. Being there was my safe place, and I knew I was in good hands with her. In her church, there were many other youth like me, and I looked forward to the discussion sessions with like-minded people. I didn't feel so awkward knowing that I could finally express my love for Christ openly and be understood in the process.

Throughout the summer, we would often go get blue crabs. I can almost smell the aroma of them cooking now. She would boil them with a special seasoning that I wish I could get now but even then, I never knew where she would buy it from. It came in a plastic tie bag and was a mixture of Old Bay and a ton of other herbs and spices. Her secret was to put a can of beer in the crabs while boiling, but she would never go buy the can of beer herself because she didn't want "her good to be evil-spoken of," as she would often say. Sometimes, she would get a can from the next-door neighbor, but if she couldn't get one from him, she would ask someone to go buy it for her. It didn't matter to me. I knew she was using it for cooking, but that wasn't the point. She would explain that people would make assumptions and because she was a leader in the church and a junior high school teacher, she didn't want any problems.

On the evening of my sixteenth birthday, when we arrived back home, there were a few guys on bikes not far from her house. I immediately locked eyes with one of them and he smiled, and I smiled back. I was definitely intrigued because he was dark-skinned, tall and slim. I guess you could say he was "my type." He got off the bike and started talking to me, and I since I thought he was cute, I wanted to hear what he had to say. Not long after that, I gave him my phone number and introduced him to my aunt. From that night, we were inseparable.

At that time, he was a Mormon. He expressed that he followed the faith because he said he had been in trouble as a youngster and a gentleman had taken him under his wing, which compelled him to behave and do well ever since. I'm not one to knock other religions, but I did know that the Mormon faith believed in things that were quite different from Christianity. I wanted him to know the truth and at least have something to research himself to make a sound decision.

My aunt helped me find some literature to share with him, and when I did, he was interested in knowing more. I invited him to the youth Bible study that I attended and that night, he gave his life to Christ.

When we first started dating, everything was great. We saw each other daily, and he attended church with me regularly.

Soon, the summer was drawing to a close. My hope was that I would continue to stay with my aunt. Unfortunately, a time in my life that was so grounded and beautiful became ugly and miserable.

My aunt sat me down and told me that my mom had demanded that I come back home. Of course, I didn't want to go back. I was finally in a place of peace and had no intentions of going back. My aunt had offered to take me to school daily since she taught at the junior high school down the street from my high school. She told me that she tried to assure them that she would make sure I went to school and went on to college if my mom let me stay, but she refused.

She hated the fact that things were going well for me at my aunt's house, and instead of doing what was best for me, she let her jealousy of my relationship with my aunt cloud her judgment. She even threatened that if I didn't return home before a certain time, she would put me in juvenile detention. I can honestly say that I disliked my mother to the point of borderline hatred. There were so many times when she would do things just to aggravate me, and I often looked at her more as an immature non-friend than a mother figure.

I remember crying so badly when I had to go back to her house. I vowed that I would leave and immediately put my plan into place.

I was working as an assistant at a salon at the time, and I used my money to purchase home goods every day I went to work. My goal was to get out of there as soon as possible, and nothing was going to stop me.

School started in September, the day after Labor Day. One night in October, my mom had come into my room and saw all the boxes I had been packing. She asked what was in the boxes, and I told her it was the things for my apartment. She told me that I needed to put the things in the attic to take to college, but I knew I was moving.

At that point, she called my stepdad in and after some discussion, he determined that I needed to move out by November 30. That was great for me. I didn't want to come back in the first place. My boyfriend and I had been talking about things, and we planned to move in together.

When November 30th came, I moved as planned, but our apartment wasn't ready, so I had to move to my other aunt's house temporarily. She wanted me to stay with her, but I knew I didn't want to stay with her. We had an amazing relationship but living with her would not have been the best decision.

Finally, our apartment was ready. I moved and initially things were great. Rent was super cheap, so his supervisor job at Wendy's and my job at the salon was enough to sustain us. Back then, we rode the bus, biked or walked everywhere, so it didn't matter. All I was looking for was peace and simplicity.

It wasn't too long until I saw his dark side. He had a temper. He would try and argue and when I didn't indulge in the arguing, he would get angry and demand that I listen to what he had to say. I would walk away and basically have him "talk to the hand," and he hated that. I had lived in a house where there was hollering and discord, so I definitely didn't feel like dealing with that in my own house.

Sometimes, he would grab both of my arms, leaving scratches or bruises, but the first time of many when he actually hit me left me in shock.

We were leaving the movie theater at Newmarket South and were in the parking lot. I don't remember why he was angry, but he was mad because I was trying to avoid the argument by walking away. Before I knew it, he had slapped me so hard in my face that all I could feel was stinging and numbness at the same time.

Prior to that, I had been slapped in my face by both my dad and stepdad, and having my boyfriend do it put me into a fit of rage. I do not believe in a woman being slapped in the face by any man. A man's strength against a woman is unmatched; therefore, slapping a girl or woman in the face at any time is unacceptable.

All I remember in that moment was going berserk. I never allowed him to hit me or beat me. I ALWAYS fought back. No matter what, I tried to defend myself. Each time he hit me, he would cry and tell me he didn't mean it. He would also beg for forgiveness each time.

The initial slap turned into more frequent and more aggressive behavior. My father used to abuse my mother and stepmother, and I couldn't believe I had found myself in the same situation.

After months of fighting and making up, I moved out into my own apartment. I was seventeen. I figured the space may help us. I did care for him deeply and his apologies seemed sincere. Several months went by and we got back together. He promised he wouldn't hit me again and assured me that he loved me.

For a while, things were okay. I thought he had finally come to a point where he wouldn't get aggressive. Again, something set him off, and we were fighting again. One time, my mom came over to my apartment and he fought me in front of her. I remember him choking me and spitting in my face before I was able to get the strength to get up and hurl an entire knife set towards him. He had crossed the line by fighting me in front of my mother, but he didn't care. We had broken up during most of my senior year in high school, but he wouldn't take no for an answer. I had a date for prom that was quickly sabotaged by him. Mysteriously, my date's mother's car window was shattered with a brick the night before my prom. I never had proof that he actually did it, but we had a good idea that it was probably him.

After that, I couldn't take it anymore. I knew there was not going to be a change. It seemed like I couldn't escape him. I was focused on finishing school and after graduation, I was headed to basic training and advanced training in the Army National Guard.

When I got back from training, I started working in the salon again. I had gotten settled into my new apartment, and I started attending college. It wasn't long after I got back home that he found out I was back. I wasn't interested in having a relationship with him, yet he continued to beg for forgiveness, ensuring that he had changed.

There was a new barber who had started working at the salon I was working in. He was so fine, and besides being a barber, he

33

was a security guard too. Something about him made me feel safe, so we started dating soon thereafter.

My ex was still lurking around. He used to stalk me on levels that were not normal. Even though I had made it a point not to share my address, he found me. I would come home, and he would be waiting in between the buildings and would jump out at me, scaring me half to death. He would continue to beg for forgiveness and beg to have me back, but I was afraid of him.

One night, I went to stay over at my boyfriend's house, and he showed up on his doorstep asking to speak to me. Of course, I wasn't going to go to the door, and my boyfriend quickly got rid of him. I thought it was over. That night as we slept, I got a phone call around one in the morning. It was my mother asking me to come home to my apartment because something was wrong. I quickly drove to my apartment to find that it had been ransacked. I had a waterbed at the time and it had been slashed. All the water had flooded my apartment and gone into my neighbor's apartment below. My cream couches had been cut open exposing all the foam inside and dirt from my plants had been strewn all around. It was a mess. The most eerie thing about the whole situation was that my prom picture from eleventh grade had been placed on top of all the mess.

My neighbor said he had seen a black male and a white female at the house, so I immediately knew that it was my ex who had been there. Other than that description, I had no other proof. I was afraid. I was scared because no matter how many times I had reported to the police about his actions, they did absolutely nothing. I remember thinking, what will he have to do to me for them to take me seriously? He would often tell me that he would kill me before he let anyone else have me. Deep down, I believed it was possible because he was obsessed with me.

My apartment was destroyed, and I no longer felt safe living there, or anywhere alone. I moved in with my boyfriend and his roommate temporarily. Since my ex knew where his house was, we all decided to move in a high-rise in downtown Newport News.

The high-rise had security, so no one was getting in there who didn't belong. Things were fine for a while. Everything with my current guy was cool. He treated me like a queen. He was an amazing cook, and he was a charmer. He had everyone fooled. He used to buy me everything I could want, and he would buy things for my best friend. Whoever was with me, he would buy them something too. This was before they had the systems to identify bad checks. During this time, if someone wrote a bad check, they would tape the check at the register to identify the person the next time they came in. They didn't have the Lynx System back then.

He had shopped till he dropped for me, my friends, himself and his daughter. I asked about the clothes and the suits, but he claimed that some of the stuff had been in the cleaners. I remember him cooking a big seafood feast and inviting my dad and stepmom over for dinner. He was so charismatic and charming that he even had them fooled! Soon thereafter, the truth was exposed. He was a fraud. One day, while he was gone to work, I found a box of duplicate checks that had been half used. I saw that he had gone on a spending binge and in about a month's time, he had accumulated all those items. The next thing I knew, he was telling his roommate and me that he was moving to Atlanta. He had sold us on the story that his grandparents gave him a monthly stipend and that was how he was able to buy all the things he was buying. Boy, please! I knew otherwise, and he had no idea. I was ready for him to get out of there because I figured all those rubber checks were going to catch up with him sooner or later.

After he moved, letters from Atlanta started flooding the house with checks stamped with insufficient funds stamped on them. The next thing I heard was that he had been locked up in jail in Atlanta. I knew it was a matter of time before they would catch up with him.

Time went on, and I got over that fairly quickly. It was what it was, and I was just glad I knew the truth. I wasn't quite nineteen yet, so I figured I had plenty of time to date and have fun.

One day, I was at work and got a call from my ex-boyfriend's mom (not the one who had just moved to Atlanta; the one who used to hit me). I was wondering why she was calling me. She told me that her husband wouldn't let him stay there and asked if I could find it in my heart to let him crash at my place for a while. She claimed he didn't have anywhere to go and that he was homeless, and she didn't want to see him on the street. At first, I thought to myself, heck no. He didn't have anywhere else he could go? Since she was pleading, I figured a few weeks would be okay. When I look back, I don't know how I allowed this to happen. I think I felt sorry for him or something, and his mom was so sweet, so how could I tell her no? I tried to rationalize the situation. He had helped me years before when I wanted to move from my mother's house. Even though I wasn't dating him, and I no longer wanted him romantically, I didn't want to see him in the street either.

I gave him my couch to crash on; however, I did have some rules. This arrangement was strictly temporary because his mother had asked. There were to be no people in my place, and he was not to get too comfortable because the arrangement was only for a short while, so his mother could figure something out.

He had been sleeping in my couch for about two weeks before all hell broke loose. One Saturday, my best friend and her girlfriend and I decided to go to Virginia Beach. While walking the strip, my girlfriend spotted him in the car with a girl I knew he had been with when we had dated, and that's when things went left. As we yelled his name, his friend sped off. I was livid. Here I was being Miss Nice Nice letting him stay at my house while he was out hanging with the chick from the trailer park? Oh no, no, no, no! We immediately left VA Beach and drove to my apartment. The security guard told me he had just gotten there.

He was in the apartment pretending he was asleep, and I wasn't having it. By me letting him stay there, he was blocking any opportunity I had to date anyone. I wanted him out. I wanted him out immediately. My girlfriend and I started yelling at him, telling him to leave. The next thing I knew, he had lured me into my second bedroom and jumped me. My girlfriend ran into the room and jumped on his back hitting him from behind while I got up from the floor. Her girlfriend ran into my kitchen and grabbed the biggest butcher knife I had out of my drawer. As I ran out of the room, I saw him run toward her into the kitchen, and I knew what he was thinking. I made a b-line towards the door and started running down the hall. I lived on the fourteenth floor, so I was running but it felt like I was running in slow motion. The next thing I felt was the collar of my shirt being pulled from behind, and he was instantly on top of me, panting with glazed out eyes looking down at me. It took all the strength I had in my body to try to hold the knife back. As he pushed downward, I pushed upwards. I was pushing back with all the strength I had in my body. Our hands were shaking, and I knew if I didn't hold on, the knife would plunge deep into my heart. I begged and pleaded with him constantly repeating his name over and over and over. He was gone, an empty shell; something had possessed him in that moment.

I saw my life flash before my eyes. Everything and everyone I ever loved flashed past my eyes like a slide show on speed. I knew I was about to die. I had never seen eyes so empty in my life. He was growling like a wild animal, using both hands and his strength to pierce my heart. With everything in me, I held on for what seemed like an eternity. Then I heard it. The security guard had made his way upstairs. He coaxed him to let go of the knife and as he did, an army of police arrived and all I heard was the unanimous sound of pistols being drawn and cocked. There were at least eight officers in the hallway. Thank God for the neighbor who had called the police. God saw fit to save me. He had given me another chance. I had come so close to death, I felt it. I had briefly looked into the enemy's eyes that day because he was gone. My ex was outside of himself and something else had taken over. They arrested him and took him away, and I was stunned and numb.

I thought about how many times I had forgiven him. I thought about how many times I had let his tears and his false words that were void of sincerity permeate my ears. For every slap, he would beg and say he was sorry. But deep down, I knew he wouldn't change. I was a battered woman. How could I have allowed this to happen? Why did I go back after all those times? What was wrong with me? How could I have loved this monster? Over and over, I beat myself up for staying or for allowing him to come back into my life, even though I wasn't even with him the last time.

I realized that he wasn't the best person because of the abuse, but he wasn't the worst either. He had issues. His father battered his mother and he grew up thinking that was okay.

As women, we need to know when to get out and stay out. There are too many women dying at the hand of a boyfriend or spouse every few minutes somewhere in the world. Get out for the sake of your life or your children's lives.

Fortunately, he didn't kill me that day. My angels were surrounding me that day because in that moment, I thought I was going to die. It's okay to leave. It's okay to move on. Even though he may tell you that you're nothing and no one else can have you, and even though he has torn down your self-esteem, there is a bigger plan for your life if you would just open your eyes.

If you're in a situation that is unhealthy, I beg you to make a decision today to get out. No matter how many times he apologizes, it will not get better. You are beautiful and wonderfully made, and you will be alright.

Moments of Reflection

Are you or have you been in a situation where there was emotional or physical abuse?

_____

_____

_____

What steps will you take to get out of the situation?

_____

_____

_____

Stepping Out in Faith

Prior to my Annual Training with Design Essentials in January 2001, I had made the decision to move. I wasn't quite sure where I would move, but I knew it was time. When I mentioned it, everyone thought I was crazy. That's one of the times when I learned it was better to keep some things to myself. Between the peanut gallery and my own voice of reason, I was bombarded with a barrage of thoughts, and I needed clarity.

I went to annual training that year and instead of staying at the hotel the entire time, I rented a car, so I could explore. I had been to Atlanta a few years before, but only to visit a friend. To visit and to live there were two different things.

Since I was born and raised in Hampton, Virginia, I felt like I had come to a point that I had outgrown the area. I was successful. I had my own salon and I owned my townhouse, but I felt this nagging urge that something was bigger and better for me. I opened the salon the week of Christmas 1998. I had poured every dime I had into the place, and I had an established clientele and a fully-staffed salon, so I was in a really good place.

It wasn't long thereafter that I felt I had been called to more. What that was I didn't know. I had decided that I would look in Northern Virginia or Atlanta. If I moved anywhere, I would have to have some steady income because I would be starting over.

My first degree was in business administration with a concentration in finance, so I figured with my degree and experience with owning the salon, I would have a good shot at finding something in management.

I investigated salon management and found that Ratner Company, the owners of Hair Cuttery, were looking for managers. The recruiter interviewed me over the phone, and the next thing I knew, I was flying to Atlanta for a face-to-face interview with her. She asked where I would like to be located regionally, and to my surprise, there were openings in both Northern Virginia and the Atlanta area!

God sure has a funny way of answering prayers, and I was faced with the dilemma of where to go. The job in Northern Virginia was in Fairfax, and the position in the Atlanta area was located in the northern suburb Alpharetta.

Since both areas were unfamiliar to me, I had to do a process of elimination. When I flew in for the interview, it went so well that I was almost one hundred percent sure I had the job before I left to return home. I remember feeling a good type of anxiety more than anything. But most of all, I wanted to make sure I was making the right decision because this would ultimately affect not only my life but my children's lives too.

As I think back, I remember my uncle had flown in from Tanzania to preach at a local church that was located across the street from my salon. I hadn't seen him in many years, and I wanted to support him, so I decided I would attend at least one night. Little did I know that it was a divine appointment to hear him speak. I believe it was a revival of some kind because he preached three nights in a row, and although I had only planned to attend one night, I found myself rushing to get out of the salon to get there. Night after night, I was glued to the edge of my seat waiting with baited breath to see what he would say next.

It was as if no one else was there and the sermon was tailor-made just for me. I remember him talking about how he was a little boy sitting on my grandmother's front porch watching planes in the air and wishing he was on them. I used to feel the same way. I always wanted to travel and experience different things, and I was never afraid of adventure.

He knew he was different. He knew there was more, and when he talked about how God had called he and my aunt to Africa for ministry, I was clear in that moment that it was time for me to go.

One thing that he said that I have applied to every daunting decision since is, "Don't be afraid to jump out into the Jordan at high tide. Be like Nike and just do it." Wow! That was so powerful! Something as simple as that impressed upon my heart so much that I have made that my personal mantra by which I live on a daily basis.

I have what one would call "crazy faith." I believe I can do anything and everything I want when I put my mind to it. Another thing he said was, "God will place an enabler to enable you to do everything you need to do." He said that everywhere I would step, things would be worked out.

Of course, that sounded great and for some, it was easier said than done. However, with a little encouragement, I was on my way. He didn't know how much the sermon impacted me. He had no earthly idea that he was the catalyst that helped propel me into that next chapter of my life.

After the sermon, he was out in the hall receiving people, and I shared with him the fact that I wanted to move and that I had been considering the two areas. My biggest fear was that I was a single mother at the time, and I would be moving to an area where I had no support system. I really didn't know anyone in Atlanta and at the time, my boys were very young.

As I explained to him how I didn't have a babysitter and how I didn't know anyone, he stopped me in my tracks. As I was finding excuses, he was telling me how I could do it. I felt empowered and unafraid.

That night, I bought the cassette tape of the sermon, and I listened to it over and over and over until I had almost memorized it.

The morning I flew to Atlanta before my interview, I had the sermon on repeat the entire flight down. I truly believe that is why my interview went so well. I had so much confidence walking into that interview that I knew I had the job from the onset of our conversation.

It was only a few days later that I got the call with the job offers. As I said earlier, God has a funny way of answering prayers. I not only had one offer, I had two! I was offered the position of assistant salon leader in Fairfax and salon leader in Alpharetta.

Living in Fairfax would be very expensive, and I wasn't certain the assistant position offered enough to sustain me. But most of all, I would still be in Virginia, so I didn't feel like it was a really big move. It was the safe move. I was still close to Hampton, and I felt a tug in my heart for Atlanta. I really didn't know what to expect moving there, I just knew that I wasn't going to be afraid in doing so.

I decided that by June 1, 2001, I would be in Atlanta. I had to give the recruiter a definitive answer, so June was my official transition time.

Since I had never been to Alpharetta before, I had no idea where I would decide to live. I quickly learned that the lower exit numbers off Georgia 400 meant that I would be closer to Atlanta, and the higher numbers meant I was north of Atlanta closer to Cumming, GA. Therefore, by process of elimination, I was able to narrow my list down fairly quickly. Being closer to Atlanta equated to more traffic, and I wasn't too thrilled about having to deal with that.

I searched online on forrent.com and asked some of my existing clients which areas were best. I had also picked up a few rental books while in Atlanta that January, so I had a few visuals to refer to as well.

Every now and again, a little fear and maybe even doubt crept into my mind, but I kept those thoughts at bay because I knew I was making the right decision. I narrowed my search to a few nice places and to my surprise, I did have some initial sticker shock. I found out very quickly that rent was quite expensive in Atlanta and in its surrounding areas, and on top of that, things were spread out pretty far apart as well. It literally takes at least 30-40 minutes to travel anywhere around the area, unlike the ease of home where everything is about 15-20 minutes apart.

As I was searching for my apartment, I had narrowed the search down between 2 apartments. As I stated earlier, God will place an enabler to enable you to do whatever you need to do. The day I called the rental office, I connected with a young lady who actually became my first client and longtime friend. The apartment was beautifully appointed and centrally located in Alpharetta, and I didn't have to get on the interstate at all to get to my new job, which was a plus in itself.

As I made my way to Atlanta, I was excited and nervous at the same time. I had peace that I couldn't explain. So many people had their two cents to put in about my move. Some were happy, and others tried to deter me for their own selfish reasons. My dad in particular couldn't understand why I would leave my salon and townhouse behind, but I didn't expect him to understand. He barely traveled outside of Hampton Roads himself and to my knowledge, has only ventured to Maryland and back. I didn't care what anybody had to say. It was my move, and I was geared up to see what was in store for me.

The kids had at least two weeks of school left at the time, so I enlisted the help of my family to take care of them while I adjusted to my new home in Alpharetta. I drove down on the first of June as planned.

Prior to leaving Virginia, I was dating a guy who would later become my husband, but I'll address that later. What is most significant about this part of my story and what I really want to drive home is the fact that one must listen to the small voice within when making life-altering decisions. Some call the voice "the voice of reason" or "the sixth sense," but I call my voice the Holy Spirit. I am the first to admit that I haven't always listened to that inner voice, and I have come to the conclusion that as a result of not listening, I have learned many hard lessons.

I've heard that hindsight is 20/20, and I would have to agree that is true. What I realized after the fact was that my move to Atlanta was for me. Notice I said for *me*; it was not for anyone else. The boyfriend and I had broken up before my move to Atlanta. He had moved to New Jersey with his sister, and I was okay with it because we had our share of ups and downs and I was eager for a new start.

As women, we need to know when to let go. We need to know that it is okay to walk away from things that are no longer serving us. I have been guilty in the past, but through various experiences, I have learned not to waste my time and energy, because continually subjecting oneself to the same foolishness is insanity in itself.

I know you're wondering why I'm saying all this. Well, I was home free. We had broken up, and I was on my way to a fresh start for my sons and me. We had the salon together, but the goal was to sell the shop, split the proceeds and move on. Obviously, that's not what happened.

I moved on June first because I was supposed to start my two-week training as salon leader, and just a few days in, he and I had started talking on the phone again, and the next thing I knew, he was knocking at my door. He had told me that his dad was driving through the area and wanted to stop and see me. I loved his dad, so I gave him my address and instead of his dad knocking at the door, it was him and his cousin. I was taken a little by the gesture, but before I knew it, my time of self-discovery and exploration of my new city turned into him and his cousin coming to stay along with his cousin's and his daughters. There went my summer of freedom. Deep down, I knew I didn't want him there, but for some reason, I couldn't muster up the words to say anything.

His cousin was an alcoholic. He could drink a cube case of beer by himself in two days. Inside, I started building resentment. I felt trapped and obligated, and it showed because I was annoyed and irritated on a daily basis. I was angry at myself for allowing it to happen and honestly, I was in utter dismay as to how I had allowed it to happen. Because I didn't have the guts to say no for whatever reason, my summer of discovery and quiet time for me turned into a three-ring circus. I realized that my decision was driven by emotions and not logic. I also realized that the obligation I felt was a direct product of the fact that he had helped me a few years earlier by buying out my former business partner. Because of my decision not to say no to this new life that had been abruptly thrown upon me, there were many disagreements, underlying resentment and of course, I felt that he had been insensitive and selfish by bringing his cousin in the first place. My space had been invaded upon and I was the one paying $1375 for rent and frankly, I wasn't excited about sharing my space. I honestly feel the story would have turned out a little differently had it just been my boyfriend and his daughter, but he couldn't see that.

Finally, he took the cousin and the cousin's kid home, which meant I had some level of peace. I was questioning myself because I couldn't understand how it all came about in the first place. Of course, I didn't mind his daughter being there, but I had ended up with a house-full. Because his daughter was young, and the cousin's daughter ended up not being old enough to babysit, that meant he had his niece come with her three kids to watch the other two. I had inherited a whole grown man, his kid, a niece and her three kids! Let's do the math. My tranquil summer turned into a house full of extra people—eight to be exact! My own children had not slept in their beds, and I had red Kool-Aid stains on my brand-new carpet because I had a house full of kids who were not mine. I kept asking myself how

I allowed myself to get into that situation, and I could only blame myself in the end.

Again, I ask, why do we stay longer than we should when things are no longer serving us?

Despite everything that was going on, I had many signs that I had made the right decision in moving. I hadn't even put an advertisement in the paper for the sale of my salon and one day, while walking in the mall, I got a call out of the blue from one of my stylists that someone was interested in purchasing the salon. I had already rented my townhouse out so that was one thing less I had to worry about. I was on my way, and I was excited about it.

Before I had secured the position with Hair Cuttery, I had negotiated terms that I would commute every other weekend to Virginia to maintain my clientele until I sold the shop. This was especially important since the take home pay from Hair Cuttery was about $500 per week at the time. Basically, I felt like I had to commute initially because I still had my financial obligations in Virginia in addition to my new rent of $1375, which almost tripled that of my $540 mortgage at home amongst other things.

The income I made was a shock too. I was used to making at least $1200 to $1700 per week at the time, so in the beginning, I felt like I didn't have an option whether to go home or not to maintain my bills. Luckily, the salon sustained itself. I had other stylists there who paid booth rent, so my salon bills were covered, and with my contribution, everything was working out well.

At least I thought everything was fine. As I settled into my new life, I noticed that every time I went home, I encountered some level of resistance. I used to fly home every other Friday on the same 10:50 pm flight on Air Iran. Initially, all was well. I would fly in, work in the salon early Saturday and part of Sunday then return home. I did this well into October of 2001. The problem was, I had listened to God tell me that it was time to move, yet I was not displaying that I truly had faith because I felt that I had to go home to be sustained. The more I went home, the crazier things got.

As months passed, I found myself going home yet dreading being there. As soon as I landed, I'd go to the salon, finish my clients and try to get an earlier flight home. I couldn't stand being there. Then, I remember driving once to pick up my sons right before school started, and on my way back, I was so tired, I got into an accident because I fell asleep at the wheel. Then September 9/11 happened. The 9/11 attack happened on a Tuesday, and I was to fly out on that Friday. The night I flew out was so unnerving because there was hardly anyone in the airport. I remember being on the train to my terminal by myself that night. I got on the plane per usual, but when we were near Patrick Henry Airport, I could feel the plane begin to circle in the air. The pilot came on the intercom and let us know there was too much fog to land, and he was unable to land at the Richmond or Norfolk airports due to the same situation.

Therefore, he had to take us to Washington/Dulles. All wasn't lost, I thought to myself. They claimed they would get us there and provide transportation back to Newport News. Now of course, I felt that was a bit inconvenient, but at least I was going to make it in time for my first client at 6:30am. Or so I thought.

We landed in Washington, and the signal to get up and offload sounded. However, the flight attendant came on the intercom and told us we couldn't get off of the plane. This is when things got crazy. The captain came on afterwards and told us we were unable to get off of the plane because the airport didn't have any security there. Now, that was the most asinine thing I had heard in my life. We had just gone through security back in Atlanta and we had only been sitting on the plane. We had already been screened, so what was the problem? We were informed that we had to sit back down and wait. From there, they began to refuel the plane and took us all the way back to Atlanta! I was livid and of course to this day, I feel like there was more to the story. All I could do was think to myself, "They have instruments to land in fog. Heck, they have auto pilot," but I was supposed to believe they couldn't land anywhere in close vicinity of my final destination.

On the ride home, all I could think about were the obstacles that kept arising every time I attempted to go home. When we arrived back in Atlanta, they rebooked us, and I was able to get another flight. However, my day was pretty much shot because I didn't arrive until after 11:30 am and I was supposed to start my day at 6:30am. I was able to reschedule some of my clients, but for the most part, the day was over. As I look back, the signs were on the wall, but I didn't want to see them. I had clearly heard the voice to move, yet I hadn't completely stepped out in faith because I was still holding on. I was not allowing God to do what He wanted to do in my life because I was too busy trying to orchestrate the plan on my own. In my mind, I felt that was what I needed to do instead of trusting the process.

I flew home on September 28th without incident; however, the beginning of October proved to be the moment when I had to make a clear and final decision. I attempted to fly home yet another Friday evening. I parked my car at the Sandy Springs Train Station and caught the Marta to the airport. When I got there, I saw a sea of people stretched far into the Atrium of the airport and my heart sank. I knew there was no way I would get through all those people to make my flight on time. One of the airport workers must have read the despair on my face and offered to put me in a wheelchair to jump to the front of the line. I refused. I couldn't allow myself to do it. All I could think to myself was that I would end up in a wheelchair permanently for getting in one illegitimately. Yet again, I was stuck. I was so annoyed and angry about the situation that I went to the AirTran counter and demanded my money returned. Then I marched out of the airport, took the train back to my car and proceeded to drive to Virginia. I was driving on pure adrenaline. I angrily shut my cellphone off and drove the entire time practically in silence because I was stewing so much, I couldn't think straight. When I arrived around 5:30 in the morning, me bestie and my boyfriend were so upset with me because I had just been in an accident a couple of months before on that drive and my actions of turning my phone off and being unresponsive were inconsiderate on my part. They were worried sick, and I felt bad about it. I was so caught up in my own feelings that I had not considered anything or anyone else around me.

I made it to the salon, but I was exhausted. That Sunday afternoon, instead of going back to Atlanta, we were headed on a cruise to the Bahamas with some of my family. During those 5 days, I had to ask myself if it was worth it. Was it worth all the hassle I had been going through all those months? The funny thing is, each time I went back to Virginia, there was some type of obstacle in the way. What I realized was, I had been operating in my own will, and I truly was not exhibiting the faith that I claimed I had because I was trying to do everything in my own power. In my mind, I felt I had to go home to make ends meet, but if that were the case, why did I move in the first place if I was going to hold on to the very thing that I moved from? On that cruise, I realized I had not been operating in faith. I was doing what I always did. I was blocking my blessing by trying to make it work my way.

When I got back from the cruise, I went to the salon for what would be my last bi-weekly commute. I packed the remainder of my things from my salon and went back to Georgia. I knew in that moment why it worked out that I had driven as opposed to flying, and I knew that officially letting go would help me to truly exercise my faith and prepare my heart and mind for what was in store for me. I eliminated the distractions and allowed myself to embrace my new life wholeheartedly.

One of the greatest revelations I had after making the final decision to let go was when I actually did, things began to prosper like never before. I stayed at the Hair Cuttery for about eight months. I was right in the heart of Alpharetta near an affluent community called St. Ives. While working there, I began to meet many women. At that time, there were not many African Americans who lived in that area, and the ones who did, were married to ball players and executives. There was a Harris Teeter grocery store next door to the salon. As they passed to go to the grocery store, they would see me in the front through the window and stop in. I began to grow my clientele fairly quickly and before I knew it, I was generating more money than I had before.

It was also suggested to me by at least three of my clients that I look into working closer to the city. They assured me that with my talent, I would make a considerable amount money that would be far more than I was presently receiving. It was time to move and step out again. I inquired about the salon Nseya in Sandy Springs and soon thereafter, I got the job and started working there. I had planned to at least stay for a year, but due to some of their salon practices, I ended up leaving after ten months. The next move was back into working for myself. I can be honest and tell you that I hated commission. After having my own salon and working for myself since I was eighteen as a booth renter, I was not too keen on giving up 45% of my money. I knew how it worked, and I was ready to get back out there on my own. I had built my clientele and I knew with a minimum of thirty steady clients, I would be able to sustain myself.

Finally, I moved that last time to my own business that I still have until this day. In the Spring of 2002, I moved to a salon suite and opened my own business called Flawless Sessions Hair Salon. My salon in Virginia was called Flawless Unisex Hair Salon, so I didn't want it to have the same name. From that point, my business started to soar. I was consistently making more than I had ever made working in Virginia or at the Hair Cuttery, and I had stopped trying to commute home at that time too. Things were looking up for me and what I realized was when I was operating in my own will, things were a struggle. As soon as I started operating in God's will, things began to line up for me.

For every step I took, I remembered what my uncle told me. "Don't be afraid to step out in the Jordan at high tide. Be like Nike and just do it!"

This new life of mine took some commitment and effort, but in the end, I never had regrets and am still loving my life in the "A."

Moments of Reflection

What decisions are you making out of obligation?

_____

_____

_____

What are you holding on to that is no longer serving you?

_____

_____

_____

What moves do you want to make, and why haven't you made them?

_____

_____

_____

Precious Gifts

I believe one of the most beautiful honors is that of becoming a mother. I never knew how important the charge was until I became one myself. Oftentimes, I still look at my children in awe and say to myself, "Wow, they came from me!" That alone is amazing in itself. As I look at my children, I am thankful that I was entrusted with their lives, and I don't take that lightly.

When I was fourteen years old, I decided that I didn't want kids. I had vowed that I would try and have my tubes tied, work, shop and travel for the rest of my adult life. Due to my circumstances, that is how I felt at the time.

It wasn't until I became pregnant the first time that those thoughts changed. I was initially very happy yet scared at the same time. I'm not sure if one is ever really ready, no matter what their age. No matter how much planning you do, there is always some underlying apprehension about it all.

I remember I didn't really say much to a lot of people about it. I didn't have morning sickness. Instead, I would get sick at night. Is there even a such thing as night sickness? Anyway, I was working and going to school, doing my normal routine. I didn't feel like I was doing anything out of the ordinary, and then it happened.

One afternoon, I felt slight cramping. It wasn't excruciatingly painful, but I did feel cramping. I had just made it to my ninth week and up until then, all had been well. I had read books and heard stories from others that slight cramping or discomfort in the beginning was normal, since my uterus was beginning to grow with the growth of the baby. Initially, I had no worries because I thought it was normal. As time progressed, the cramping became worse and I was buckled over in pain with what seemed like the worst menstrual cramps one could have. The next thing I knew, I started bleeding. That's when I knew something was wrong. I remember going to the bathroom and seeing all this and not knowing what to do.

I called my doctor and they asked me to come in. That was the longest ride for me, even though it was really just around the corner. When I arrived, the nurse had me undress and lay down on the table. Since I was so early, they had to do an internal ultrasound and the dreaded words I didn't want to hear parted my doctor's lips. "I can no longer find the baby," he said. I was numb. I felt like I had been hit with a sledgehammer. One minute I was fine embracing the fact that I was going to be a mother, and in that instant, I was without child, mourning the loss of a special person I would never know. I was devastated. I played the scenario over and over wondering if it were something that I did wrong or could have done differently for that matter.

I wanted to wake up out of this terrible nightmare, but I was awake. It was true, the precious life that I had begun to carry was no more.

I was really sad. I blamed myself, thinking I had done something wrong and as time passed, I grew to accept it. As a woman of faith, I did question God, but I found some peace in it all because I was told that He knew best and that maybe the baby wasn't developing properly. The older women told me it was His way to spare me additional heartache if something were to be wrong with the baby if it had made it to full-term. That did help some, but it was the wondering "if" that constantly ran through my mind.

The second time I became pregnant was almost three years later. I was working full-time and taking a couple of evening classes at Thomas Nelson. I didn't really have morning sickness but again, I had night sickness. Luckily, it wasn't every night, but I did have sickness at night from time to time.

Speaking from experience, when you lose a baby once and get pregnant again, you always find yourself counting the weeks up to and past the time that you had the last miscarriage. Therefore, when I had made it to nine weeks, that was a win for me. My first angel didn't make it past nine weeks, and I remember as I approached the nine-week mark, I was extra cautious. I didn't want to do anything out of the ordinary.

Nine weeks came and went. I had made it past that dreadful milestone in my mind. I had always been told that if you make it past your first trimester, you were pretty much out of the woods. Well, then it happened. I was driving and felt the sharpest pain run through my body. Then, it felt like my water had broken but instead it was blood. I could feel my jeans getting wetter and I knew what was happening.

I immediately drove straight to my doctor's office and as I was laying down on the table staring at the ceiling, everything became a blur. The sounds around me were loud yet distant, and it felt as though I was no longer in my body. I found myself going through the same scenario as I had before, just three years earlier, and I was in utter disbelief. How could I tell my boyfriend that I was no longer carrying our child? We had been so happy imagining what our little one would be and making plans for our future.

I was 11.5 weeks, and my precious baby was gone. How could this be happening again? What was wrong with me? Why had this happened yet again? I was beyond devastated. This time around, I had told many people. I remember my boyfriend's mother being so happy when we told her we were expecting, and then we had to tell her we were weren't. It was so hard. I cried for a while. I was empty. I felt like I had no purpose, like that part of me as a young woman was somehow flawed and broken. I had told many of my clients and after losing the baby, it was so hard when they came back in to get their hair done because I would have to tell them that the baby was gone.

I was going through a lot of emotions. I was really afraid that maybe my words of young had come back to haunt me. Somehow, I felt that my declaration at fourteen years old had somehow cursed me for my future. I felt like a failure. I knew I could conceive, but I was having obvious trouble carrying to full-term. Since I was young, I think my doctor felt I had time to try again. However, I was afraid. I was afraid that I would never be able to have children and now that I was older, my desire to have children had changed. I wanted a little girl so badly, I would often dream about her. I was determined not to give up. Having lost two already, I regained the strength to try again. I was not going to wallow in pity and self-defeat.

When I got pregnant for the third time, I was nervous, yet quietly confident that things would be okay. Week 9 came and went. Week 11.5 came and went. I had made it past those two pivotal points, yet I was still nervous. This time, I didn't want anyone to know. I was afraid to tell just in case my body failed me again. I didn't want the hurt, shame and guilt I felt when I had lost the other two, so I was reluctant to share with anyone, even though it was a joyous occasion.

I had reached 16 weeks without incident. I was so happy I didn't know what to do. Becoming a mother was finally setting in and was within my reach. My belly continued to grow, and I started to feel the welcomed kicks within. I later found out that I was having my first son. Initially, I was upset because I wanted a girl, but I had to check myself and be thankful that whatever I had would be a healthy blessing from God.

After 24 hours of labor, my beautiful son entered the world. I was so happy! Two years and ten months later, I gave birth to his brother and at the end of 2003, I was blessed with their baby sister. Although I had lost two initially, God saw fit to allow me to have three of my own children. I know that having a child is a miracle, and I will never take that for granted.

Despite what things looked like, I never gave up faith that I would one day safely bring a child into the world. If you have ever been in my situation or are going through troubles with conceiving and carrying to full-term, I encourage you to not give up or give in. In the way that God sees fit for you, it will happen. Maybe you will carry your child. Maybe you will have to enlist the help of a surrogate. Maybe you will adopt or become a stepmother. Whatever way it happens, don't take it lightly because God will not put more on you than you can handle, and what is for you is for you. Be encouraged and respect the process. Know that everything happens for a reason, and there are no mistakes.

Moments of Reflection

If you have lost a child have you found yourself blaming yourself?

_____

_____

_____

If you have found yourself unable to conceive and carry to full-term, list the steps you are taking to ensure you remain emotionally whole throughout the process.

_____

_____

_____

You Are Enough

As women, oftentimes we question whether we are enough. I would venture to say that every woman I personally know has asked herself that question at least once in her life. It could have been brought on by a failed relationship or by the pursuit of a new relationship with the fear of rejection looming over head. It could have been teasing or bullying in school. Whatever the case may have been, we all have been there at some time or another.

When thoughts of not being enough enter our heads, something happens. That is when the first prick into our self-esteem occurs. Before long, it becomes a gaping hole, and we've lost ourselves and no longer know who the woman is in the mirror. You even become unknown to those around you.

I spent approximately nine years with my ex-husband including friendship, courtship and marriage. When we met, I can say that I was my most authentic self. I was confident, vibrant, always outgoing and free. As I looked back years later, I could see that while in that relationship, I had changed drastically.

After the relationship was over, one of my beautiful clients said to me one day, "Wow, Alicia, you really are cool after all!"

"Huh? What did that mean?" Was I mean? Was I quiet? I just needed to know what that meant. She went on to explain that I wasn't mean or anything, I was just different. I wasn't engaged, and I looked stressed like something was on my mind all the time.

I cried in that moment. I didn't know that I was projecting that on the outside. I apologized yet I was thankful that she had pointed it out because it gave me a chance to work on me and to pay attention more.

I had lost myself in that relationship, and it was totally unhealthy. I remember when I first started seeing him, my mother made a comment in passing that I should have listened to then. She asked me if I thought he could have been a little controlling and of course, I didn't think so. I just took it as him being romantic and loving when he would tell me to "come home now and stop what I was doing because he just wanted me to come home." Who knew that it would grow into other things down the line?

So, let's take it back to the beginning. When we met, I used to wear my hair many different ways. I actually had a weave in at the time. I'm a hairstylist until I die, so I'm expected to change my hair like the weather. I always changed my hair quite a bit as far as I can remember.

When it was time for me to take the weave out. I remember him being scared to see what I looked like because I think he thought I didn't have any hair of my own. I had plenty of hair. I just wanted it different at times and the weaves gave me options. Now I'm not silly to think that some guys don't care for weaves, but what I do know is, if he met me that way, why would he try to change me?

As time passed, he always wanted me to wear my hair in a straight, plain bob. When I looked back at pictures during that time, I saw that I had my hair in a plain Jane bob for about four years straight. He just wanted it that way. If I did try to change my style, he would say hurtful things to me like, "I'm not attracted to you with your hair like that." So, I started to wonder if the way I wore my hair defined how much he did or did not love me. I felt trapped. I felt trapped in my own body because I didn't have the freedom to be me. His ex used to wear a press and curl. That worked for her. She was definitely a more conservative woman than me so if that's what he wanted, he should have stayed with her. I'm definitely not conservative! I felt like a caged bird. Slowly but surely, it had started. He had started to chip away at my self-confidence and my self-esteem. This was truly unhealthy. When you're in it, you don't see it. When you try so hard to please, it also leads to underlying resentment.

I found myself resenting him on levels I never knew I could. In every aspect, he tried to change me. "I don't like your hair like that. I don't like this outfit or that outfit. Your breasts are too big. I don't like the tattoos. I don't like the weave. I don't want my wife to have a navel ring. Why do you have to be on the phone when you come home?" On and on and on he would run his mouth. I just wanted to scream and tell him to shut up, along with some other choice words. There is but so much one can take. I really didn't "like" him as a person because he was very critical and the things he said were hurtful. Surely, this couldn't be a man who loved me for me. If he did, he wouldn't have tried to pick me apart and judge me on so many occasions.

I have tattoos. When I met him, I had two. I'm an artist and they are placed indiscreetly, and I loved them, or I would not have had them put on me in the first place. He complained about that. He didn't have any and that was his prerogative; however, I had had mine for years prior to meeting him. Do you know that even after we were long divorced, I had another one placed on my back and he came to get our daughter one day and had the nerve to comment about it? I just looked at him sideways! Boy, please!

Finally, I wanted a navel ring. I had wanted a navel ring for many years prior to meeting him. Again, he had something to say about that. He didn't want his wife to have a navel ring. Okay. That was a fight, but in 2005, I got one anyway. I was beginning to check out mentally and honestly, I was acting out by cutting my hair because I knew it would piss him off. So that's when my resentment was building.

Years later, long after our divorce, I was able to tell him exactly how I felt. He wasn't my ideal mate, but I loved him for him. My type is a dark-skinned guy. I like chocolate! I always have and always will! My daddy is a dark-skinned, chocolate man, so what can I say? I also like men who are physically fit. He never fit that bill. I like washboard stomachs and a basketball or football kind of build, and he was never that! In fact, he had a stomach that grew from a 36 waist to a 40 something at the end of it all. That stomach wasn't attractive at all; however, I never said anything derogatory about it until after we were divorced, and I was letting him know how he made me feel over the years.

In the marriage, I had lost myself. I kept trying to please him. I doubted if I was even good enough. I had never in my life lost my confidence in myself until I was with him. I thought if I changed into what he wanted, he would love me more. Surely, he will love me if I did this. Maybe he will love me if I do that? I must have been out of my mind when I think about it. I was so determined to be what I thought he wanted me to be that I lost Alicia. I no longer knew who I was when I looked in the mirror, and that was a miserable place to be.

During the marriage when I became angry at him, I would cut my hair. Cutting my hair liberated me but would infuriate him, and I knew it. What was he going to do, leave me? Well, there were many points at that time that I didn't care. He would reluctantly tell me that it looked nice. But the thing is, I knew it looked nice because I had worn short hair off and on since I was twelve! He tried to convince me that my face was too long to wear short hair. As I'm writing this, I'm laughing because he was really nuts! Thank God I am free from that foolishness!

It wasn't until we were separated, and I had found some friends outside of him, that I got "me" back. I got "me" back!

When you're in it, you can't see it. When I found myself again, there was no looking back. Do you know even after we weren't together, he felt he needed to give his opinion? I went natural the first time in 2010. He had married someone else and was still running his mouth. I was wearing my hair curly and he had seen a picture of the kids and me at his mother's house. He had the audacity to tell me that wearing my natural hair made my skin look rough! What in the world did that mean? At that moment, I just laughed and thanked God for my own mind to do whatever I wanted to do because I was no longer with him. I vowed that I would never again try to change myself for a man, and I congratulated myself for not being affected by his words. What you see is what you get, and if he couldn't love me for me, then he was not the one! That's my motto!

"The one" loves me for me! "The one" lets me be me and enjoys it. He compliments me. He doesn't tear me down. He lifts me up! He encourages me! He enhances me in every way!

The funny thing that I discovered is, insecure, hurt people end up hurting others. In many ways at the time, my ex was insecure. He wasn't whole himself, so he spewed his insecurities all over me to make himself feel better. He cast self-doubt on me because he wasn't right himself. His self-esteem wasn't totally intact, so he tried to tear me down to make himself feel better. The devil is a lie! If you're in that type of situation, get out of there! Pick yourself up and get to a place where nothing or no one can tell you anything different.

You are beautiful! You are whole and complete, just how you are. Your hair, whether it's long, short, curly or straight, is just fine! Your body is just the way God made you! You are sexy! You are all that and a bag of chips! You are fabulous! Tell yourself these things and don't ever look back! If the man in your life is making you feel less than, and if you have lost your sense of identity, check him about it. If he continues to tear you down and belittle you, make a change that gets you back to a healthier state of mind. It's not healthy to feel that way. You are fearfully and wonderfully made. Who is he to say otherwise!

Moments of Reflection

Write down a time that you felt that you weren't enough.

_____

_____

How did you feel?

_____

_____

What was said or done to make you feel that way?

_____

_____

What steps did you take, or will you take, to change your circumstances?

_____

_____

Daily Affirmation

Look in the mirror every day and tell yourself, "I am enough!"

Surviving Divorce

JOHN HARRINGTON AND CHEYENNE BUCKINGHAM | 24/7 WALL STREET 7:00 a.m. EST Feb. 2, 2018

About 40% to 50% of married couples in the United States divorce, according to the American Psychological Association. The divorce rate among those who remarry is even higher.

With those kinds of statistics, it's a wonder anyone gets married or stays married at all. I was 22 when I married my son's father. Honestly, I can really only contribute the fact that we were young at the time, along with him not being ready for the responsibility of marriage, to our demise. We both wanted to "do the right thing" because we had a child out of wedlock and the pressures of those around us probably contributed to why we got married when we did. At the time, I was perfectly okay with not being married but because we were living together and had a child already, the elders had something to say. I would hear things like, "You're living in sin," or "Why are you all shacking up?" But, the moral of that story is, you shouldn't get married unless you want to or are ready to, not because family or outside pressures force you to do so.

We stayed married "on paper" for six years. Most of which we lived separate lives but he always took care of us. Always. Despite our divorce, we have remained close friends and I love him until this day because he is family. I have known him since I was nineteen years old, and he has been consistent since I have known him.

Now, that scenario doesn't play out like that for every divorcée. I was extremely lucky because we had no ill will towards one another. We were truly friends and actually divorced peacefully. "Family first" is our motto, and we've done an excellent job in co-parenting. Plus, he has been with me through all the drama, so I am extremely blessed for that. My marriage to my daughter's father is another story.

In hindsight, all the signs were there from the beginning. But as women, sometimes I think we feel we may be able to help the man in many ways, and I believe that is due to our nurturing nature.

When I met him, we became good friends and he bought my old business partner out of my business. He owned an auto shop and was in the Air Force at the time. He was also married at the time, but as he tells it, he had been unhappy for years. I am sure some of that is true, but there are always three sides to a story. Knowing what I know now, it wasn't all her and I certainly know in my situation, it wasn't all me. Now with wife number three, he is still up to the same old shenanigans.

In the beginning, he was sweet, kind and very charming. However, the charming side really equated to him being a controller and a master manipulator.

I told you earlier how we had broken up while dating and how he ended up in Georgia, which was supposed to be my move alone. I did love him, so I wanted to make things work.

One of the biggest problems we had that certainly contributed to our divorce was the fact that he was not stable when it came to holding a steady job. When we initially met, he was stable, but when he deliberately failed his PT test to get out of the Air Force, I should have known what I was dealing with then.

He had put in ten years and in another ten, he could have retired. Instead, he got out and took the payment to get out. Instead of reinvesting the money, he spent it on a BMW. Now, I am the queen of cars, but I'm just letting you see that his decision making wasn't the best.

When he moved to Atlanta, he was installing DirecTV for customers and he was making good money doing it. He was earning at least $1000 per week, which was good, especially with both of our incomes together.

The problem came when things started to slow down, and he did not like doing the job anymore. Then he went on to work as a manager at Rich's, which is now Macy's. It was an entry-level job, but it was steady money.

He started to complain that he didn't like the job and that he hated going in. I can think of many jobs that I didn't necessarily want to do, but I did them because I had to take care of my family. He told me every time he got near the job that he would get a headache or sick to his stomach. Not long thereafter, I got a call while at work and he was telling me that he didn't feel well, and I was extremely worried because he didn't sound right. He said he had been laying on the floor in the stock room at the job, and he said he was going to go to the doctor. I immediately left work and I met him at the Georgia Clinic not far from our apartment.

When I got there, he had gotten out of the car and was limping and stiff on one side, looking like he was about to fall over. I thought he had had a stroke or something. The people from the clinic rushed out to get him and placed him on the gurney in the examination room. We had gotten married not long before this happened, and all I could think was that my husband was about to die. I was truly scared. The doctor had given him aspirin and performed an EKG, and then he called an ambulance to come take him to the North Fulton Hospital because he felt the treatment he needed was beyond his scope.

We got to the hospital and they ran a ton of tests on him. He was reluctant to go, but they wouldn't release him until they could figure out what was wrong with him. Finally, they were ready to let him go home. The prognosis was that he had had a panic attack. A panic attack? Wow! I had heard that panic attacks sometimes present the same symptoms as a heart attack, but this was a lot to digest. The doctors had released him and told him he could go back to work, but he never went back. In my mind,

I certainly wanted him to be well, but since they said he was okay, I thought he would at least talk to his manager and go back to work. He never did. He needed a job. I had a client who said she may be able to help, but the initial job she offered didn't come through. In the meantime, he tried selling water softeners. After leaving the house daily for almost three weeks, there was nothing. He said the people didn't pay him for the time even though he had worked for it. After that didn't work out, he went on to something else.

The instability with his jobs certainly caused a strain on our relationship. We had a baby on the way, and I was worried that he would never settle down into something that would bring a decent income into the house. After the water softeners, he started working for Sanis by selling disposal containers to companies. He hated that too. He said he wanted to run his own business but wasn't sure what he wanted it to be. Our biggest arguments were about money and the fact that he wouldn't hold a steady job.

There were a few more jobs and businesses after that, and I had become so frustrated one day that I asked him what he had always dreamt of being when he grew up. He said he wanted to own his own business. Again, owning a business comes with a plan first and foremost. It also comes with having the resources to start one. I remember just having our baby and he was sitting on the phone with one of his friends telling him that he was wanting to know when I would let him quit his job, so he could pursue another one of his business ideas full-time.

I was all for him starting a business if that is what he wanted to do, but it made sense to keep the steady thing going on the side until the business could overtake the income the job was bringing in. Didn't that make the most sense? Why would one quit the steady thing given the fact that there were responsibilities to take care of? I couldn't understand It to save my life.

On top of the frustrations of him constantly switching jobs, I found myself growing weary of the whole situation. Day by day, I kept wondering what my life would have been like had he stayed in New Jersey and never come down to Atlanta when I initially came to the city.

As a woman, all we really want is to feel safe and secure with our men, and I felt neither from him. I didn't have the confidence in him as I should have, and I began to resent him for putting us in predicaments because he couldn't see past what he wanted to do in the moment and what he did or didn't like about the "flavor of the month" job he had at the time.

He blamed his parents for not encouraging him to go to college, but my parents hadn't encouraged me to go to college. I moved out of my parents' house at 16 and neither of my parents had graduated from college at the time, so I looked at that as an excuse. He could never take responsibility for his actions. It was always someone else's fault as to why something didn't happen for him.

When we had our daughter, I didn't have confidence then. She was born December 30th and when it was time to pay the rent on the first, he didn't have it. He had assured me that things were taken care of and instead of me enjoying my beautiful baby, I was worried how the rent would get paid.

Over and over this would happen. When he did venture out to do businesses, they always had some "get rich quick" tactic behind it. Then he would get angry with me if I didn't have buy-in to what he was doing. He would get angry and accuse me of not being supportive if I didn't want to bring my clients into what he was doing. What he failed to realize is that I had built my clientele from nothing. I had gained trust and confidence from them, and I wasn't comfortable introducing them to the multi-level marketing business he was trying to establish. It wasn't fair to me and he couldn't see that.

One time, he partnered with a young lady to do home loans and refinancing, and he wanted me to solicit my clients to do home loans and refinancing for them. I wasn't comfortable doing that because that meant he would be privy to their personal financial information, and I didn't want them to feel like we were having pillow talk about their personal information. I did turn him on to one of my clients, and they were unable to qualify, and I never saw her again. She was a faithful bi-weekly client and all of a sudden, she didn't come anymore, and I was supposed to believe it was unrelated? Please!

One thing happened after another, and I remembered in my marriage counseling during the weeks that led up to my marriage that I had the warning signs. All the reservations I had were clear in what I was expressing during the counseling sessions. The pastor asked us to write down things that we felt were important to address prior to getting married. One thing that I know I wrote down was about him changing jobs and making sure he talked to me before doing so. Long after our divorce, I sat back one day and realized that including what he does now, he had twelve different jobs during the time we were together.

He decided he would attempt to be a truck driver but couldn't do that because of his license. Not even four months later, he decided he was going to go to flight school. At that point, I just wanted him to do something and stick with it. I was tired. I had been the bread winner for our household since we had been together, and with my first husband. From the example from my grandfather, I wanted and expected my man to be the bread winner, and I never had that with him. I often regretted marrying him and I knew that I should have followed my voice. My little voice told me not to do it. I heard it clearly. Just because you love someone doesn't always mean they are the best for you.

Did we have some good times? Of course, we did. But I do know that leading causes for divorce are infidelity and money issues, and both were present in my case. When he left for flight school, I just wanted him to go because I was tired of him whining about the fact that he was unhappy at his job. I wanted him to go and find himself because I was so stressed to the point that I had begun to lose respect for him, and I resented him for being so selfish. Around the same time, I had released a gospel album and all I wanted to do was sing. I didn't go to him and tell him that I wanted to quit my job at the expense of the family to pursue my singing career. I knew that I would need to do that on the side and if it took off, so be it. That was logical reasoning. Obviously, he couldn't see that.

When he initially left, we had just closed on a house in April. He left for flight school in July. If I had known he wanted to go to flight school a few months earlier, I would not have agreed to move into the house in the first place. Our new mortgage was $2600, and with both of us working, we would have been fine. Going to flight school meant he was not supposed to be working, and even if he did, it was limited.

I had a new daycare bill of $800 per month added to the budget on top of the monthly bills at the house and at my salon. I sought to get another job because I needed an income that was fixed, so I could be reassured that all of the bills would get paid.

The strain of him being in school began to take a toll on the family as a whole. I had become a single mother even though I was married, and I began to resent my life more and more every day. I was seeking my master's degree, while working three other jobs and attending to my minor children. It was hard. Extremely hard. Sometimes, I didn't know if I was coming or going. While he was attending school, all the daily pressures were on me, and I was exhausted and angry. I would find myself sometimes falling asleep at the wheel while driving. Sometimes, I would cry myself to sleep because I didn't see a way out of my situation and I didn't feel he would understand. If I tried to express how I felt, instead of listening, the first thing he would yell out was that I wasn't being supportive. It wasn't that I didn't believe in what he was trying to do, I just needed help and maybe a little recognition that I was holding things down while he pursued his dreams.

He would pop up out of the blue to surprise me and then get angry if I would crash and sleep for the day that he was there. He was completely out of touch. He had no earthly idea what it took to do what I did on a daily basis. Honestly, as I look back, I am not sure how I did it myself. I was actually putting in about 70-80 hours per week between work and school.

As mothers, we do what we have to do. I barely got four to five hours of sleep per night. I had this beautiful home yet barely spent any time there. Then I had an unreasonable partner who couldn't relate, so I felt alone. I was so busy taking care of everyone else, and I often wondered who would take care of me?

On top of him not being financially stable, he was extremely insecure. One time he came home and accused me of having another man in our home because he was analyzing a urine stain on the bottom of the toilet seat. He claimed that the only way the drop of urine could have gotten underneath the top of the toilet seat was that a man had done it. He even told me that he saw a curly hair on the seat that surely could not have belonged to me. The hair actually came from me cutting my oldest son's hair in my bathroom and the drop of urine came from my own misdirection after having a Brazilian Wax. I was appalled and annoyed. Certainly, if I wanted to step out on him, I could have done that a long time ago. I also didn't have to subject myself to his foolishness on a regular basis if that were the case.

Time went on and things didn't improve. I grew weary and one day, I asked him if I were to have a breakdown, what he would do? He said, "I guess I would have to come home." He guessed he would have to come home? That was it! There I was working like a dog to keep everything going while he was in school in another state and "he guessed" he could come home? In that moment, I decided that I would leave my home. $2600 was not worth my life or my health. It was only a material thing, and I no longer cared one way or another. We did try to put the house up for sale, but that was around the time that the market began to bubble. No one was biting because there were other new homes being built in our neighborhood. We had it on the market but got no bites.

I found an apartment that was $1350 per month. I would be saving more than half of the money I was spending monthly and welcomed the relief. He did come home and helped me move, and I was thankful.

Not long after I moved into my apartment, he was sent to Houston, Texas. Initially, I was intrigued with the idea that he was in Houston and when we went to visit him, we considered moving there. After exploring the idea, he told me he would be able to contribute $400 towards the household per month. Moving to Houston meant I would have to start all over again, and I wasn't sure I was willing to do that. I wasn't confident that moving there would be the right decision because I would no longer have the income from my salon. I could have gotten a transfer with my second job at Express, but I was only making

43K at the time and I knew that was not going to be enough to sustain our family alone. Between his $400 and my 43K, I knew we would be having discord over money even more because that was not enough to carry a family of five. I decided not to move, and he wasn't happy about it.

That was the summer of 2007. I remember it clearly because his sister had gotten married in Philadelphia, and we attended the wedding. Normally, I would fly out to visit him in Houston, but this time, he didn't want me to go. He made up some excuse that he didn't want me to get stuck since I had to fly on standby. Just a few weeks before, he had come home for Father's Day. I had taken some time off to spend with him, but something just wasn't right. He asked out of the blue if I thought he was seeing someone else and I frankly said yes. He acted surprised by my answer, but as a woman, we know. He wasn't behaving the same way. Plus, just weeks earlier, he had gone to get a full work-up at the doctor's on my insurance. Why would he be going to get all these tests when we had been married for years? I know I had been faithful, so there should not have been anything to worry about.

Then, in July, I had knee surgery on my left knee. He was supposed to come home for my surgery but the morning of my surgery, he called to tell me he had to stay for one of his student's tests. He had known about the surgery for months and could have told his managers that he needed time off. Instead, he ended up turning it on me like he always did, by accusing me of not thinking his job was as important as mine. Needless to say, he never made it. In fact, one of my good friends came with me because I was informed they would not have done the surgery otherwise.

The afternoon I got home from the surgery, my friend and her husband came to check on me. I still hadn't heard from him. It was a total of ten days that passed before I heard from him. When I did, he wasn't even calling for me. He called my phone and asked for my three-year-old daughter. After speaking to her, he hung up the phone. In that moment, I could not believe it. I called him back and told him that I wanted a divorce.

There was no way he loved me or cared for me in my mind, and I just wanted him out of my life for good. I was embarrassed because my friends asked day after day if I had heard from him or not. I just wanted out and I felt I would never forget what he had done.

I later found out he had placed an ad on Black People Meet and met a woman he had started dating. He had obviously lied to her and posed himself as a divorced man. He had moved on to the next victim. She was desperate and gullible and even after finding out that he wasn't divorced, she claimed it was too late because she had already fallen for him.

I had mixed feelings. Part of me wanted to divorce, and the other part of me wanted to try and work it out for the sake of my daughter. Plus, I felt like I didn't want to get divorced again. At one point, he had come in town and we had gone downtown to fill out the paperwork, but we didn't do it. Since we didn't file, I put my all into trying to work it out for the next three months.

The problem was, I was trying alone. He was acting as if he were coming home on the weekends when he could. However, he was still seeing her. In fact, he was living with her, I later found out. The most hurtful thing that he did was during Christmas of 2007. He came home the day before Christmas Eve. He claimed that he had to go back to Houston on Christmas Day because he had to work a temp job that day. I begged him to stay, but he only yelled at me and told me he needed the money. Because I love Christmas so much, I cooked our Christmas dinner on Christmas Eve, so we could all be a family. On Christmas morning, I took him back to the airport, so he could go to his supposed temp job.

I found out later from him that he had actually gone to spend time with his mistress and her family for Christmas dinner. He had come clean with all of his indiscretions with this woman, and I was disgusted. I felt so stupid for giving him another chance. How could I have been so dumb? I knew that I had stayed for the sake of my family and for the commitment that I had made, but at that point, it wasn't enough. I wanted out and I wanted out immediately.

The insurmountable amount of hurt that I suffered with him was indescribable. The back and forth was unhealthy for all involved. Even after our divorce, there were times that I allowed him to come back and I really feel it was a stronghold of some kind.

A little over a year after our divorce, he married the mistress. Just four months in, he was calling me and telling me it was for the birds and that he wanted to come back home. As late as 2016, he was still asking to come back, and I could not bring myself to do it. I loved him as my child's father, but I could not get over the fact that I didn't trust him. He claimed he didn't want to be with the new wife any longer and wanted to come back to me. In my heart, I knew he had hastily moved into that other situation, but despite anything, I knew I would not be able to trust him. He was calling me even then on a cell phone she didn't know he had. How could I let him come back and fly four days a week away from home, not knowing where he was? I wasn't crazy. We both had our faults to a degree, but I know that trust was a major factor and I had none for him.

Since that conversation, he has left me alone about it, but in doing so, he has cut our daughter off too. I suggested that we be parents, and I let him know that we could be friends, but that is not the case. Because I rejected him, he stopped talking to me altogether. The sad part is that he can't separate his feeling towards me from those for my daughter. It is sad when parents do that, but he will have his day when she speaks her mind letting him know how she feels.

I am at peace with it. I know I haven't done anything to him to warrant the behavior. Therefore, he will have to face the music with his own actions. I am healed and set free from everything that was done or said to me, and I can only hope that my experiences can help the next woman who goes through what I have been through.

Moments of Reflection

What lessons can you learn from me?

1. Listen to the voice and go with your first thought.
2. Don't be wishy-washy.
3. The concerns that you have are valid ones. Don't dismiss them.
4. Know that YOU CANNOT CHANGE A MAN and his ways. He has to be mature enough to see the error of his ways and do something about it.
5. Don't stay for the children! It never works. God didn't put us on this earth to be unhappy.
6. Know your worth. Do not continue to take emotional abuse or any form of tearing down of your self-esteem.
7. Sex is overrated. It's not enough to keep a marriage going alone.
8. Go into your marriage with both as whole beings. If you have it together and he doesn't, the stress that formula causes is not worth the headache.
9. When he cheats once, and you forgive him, more than likely at some point, he'll do it again.
10. Paraphrasing Maya Angelou, when he shows you who he is the first time, believe him and run! 🏃‍♀️

Help! I'm a Single Mom!

In a perfect world, families would stay together and have households with both mothers and fathers present in the home to provide a unit to nurture their children.

As little girls, it is usually instilled that the mother is the nurturer and the father is the provider, and hopefully they will live happily ever after. Unfortunately, life doesn't always work out that way. Broken homes continue to be on the rise with more and more fathers being incarcerated or homes ravaged by infidelity and lack of commitment. It is so easy to get divorced in our microwave society with billboards posted all over the city for easy, reasonably-priced, no contest divorces. There is no fight left in this day, and though it is easy to get into a marriage, getting out proves to be more difficult, especially when children and assets are involved. Breakups can bring out the worst in the nicest people, leaving a broken home with parents at odds and children as collateral damage.

I have had one example in my life of a relationship that actually lived out the vows of "till death us do part." That example was of my mother's parents. They were together as a young couple, and after my grandfather passed in 1999, my grandmother chose to continue to live alone. They raised their children together; the idea of having a one-parent home was something my grandmother never had to face because in those days, it was not an option to divorce. In her day, couples stuck it out, no matter what. Some couples in her generation said that having children out of wedlock was frowned upon and not being married was not an option.

I had my first son at 21 years old. When he was conceived, we were not married. We did marry when he was a toddler; however, we married for the wrong reasons. I loved him dearly, but I believe he wasn't ready. We were young, and he was still finding himself. We are still very good friends, and I can say that we did a great job co-parenting after divorce because we always respected one another, and he was always an exceptional example of what a provider is supposed to be.

I know for sure that I never set out to be a single mother. There aren't too many people I personally know who intentionally set out to be single mothers.

I know from my own experience that it takes an insurmountable amount of love, dedication, work, sacrifice, prayers, patience and perseverance, to say the least. And even then, you find yourself wondering if that is even enough.

My grandmother used to say, "Mama's baby, Papa's maybe," and it didn't resonate until I found myself running the ship alone. What I do know is God will not put more on you than you can bear. That being said, I know there were times when I cried myself to sleep because I was so tired that I couldn't see straight. Nursing a sick child even though I had to get up early to go work one of my three jobs at the time was something I had no choice but to do.

If I didn't do it, who would? As a mother, I did not get to determine when my child was sick or not.

There were times that I remember everything in my pantry was a generic store brand. I had to make ends meet the best way I could, and I was determined to provide for my children, whether I had support or not. The one thing I knew is that they would never go hungry or be without as long as I could help it.

I used all of the resources I could. They didn't have health insurance when I was self-employed, so I had to get Peachcare to cover them. I was so thankful for that resource, and it was imperative that I had it because two of my children had asthma. Even when I didn't have health insurance, they did. It was non-negotiable.

After I had left my house to move into an apartment, I had to cut back on everything. I had to balance my checkbook down to the cents on a weekly basis. One time, my middle son changed the amount on his lunch check by ten dollars two weeks in a row. At first, I thought that the bank had made a mistake. I called the bank and they credited my account the ten dollars. The second time it happened, I knew it wasn't a mistake. I had written the second check on my other bank account, so I knew it could not have happened by mistake twice.

I asked my son over and over, and he denied that he had done anything wrong. I repeatedly asked him if he had changed the checks, and he continued to deny it. I was so angry and convinced that I was going to beat it out of him. Before I knew it, I had tackled him and tried to choke him. I was angry at him for lying and most of all, I was afraid because I figured if he was changing checks in middle school, what would happen next? I also had issues with him hanging with the wrong crowd. Twice he got in trouble for being in the possession of an air gun. After I caught him with the gun the second time, I called the police myself to come and pick him up. I knew if I put my hands on him, I was going to hurt him, so I figured if I called the police, they would be able to talk some sense into him.

I thought that I could have him put into some kind of scared-straight program, but the police officer told me that he would not be able to take him until he was sixteen. He was only fourteen at the time, so the best I could do was threaten him and ground him for the rest of the school year and into the summer. I went to the juvenile delinquent's home that he kept trying to hang with and told his mother that she had better get a hold on him before I did. I know I was cutting up. I had all the neighborhood kids scared of me. Yes, I became that mom. I later found out that I had the nickname of the mother who was in the "Everyone Hates Chris" sitcom. I didn't care. I was in a fight to keep my kids safe and on the right path.

It is hard raising young, black men alone. I tried to instill the fear of life in them because I knew how hard it would be in the world. Once, after my oldest son had turned sixteen, he was working at a local church near our apartment. I had always talked to my kids about respecting authority and I had prepared them in the proper way to behave if they ever encountered the police.

My son had worked that day, and I knew it was close to the time for him to get off of work. It was very cold that day, so I decided that I would go pick him up, so he did not have to walk. I felt something deep down that I could not explain. Something was different, and something didn't feel right. I tried calling him but did not get an answer. I called again and again to no avail. I knew that sometimes he had a hard time getting a signal on his phone since where he worked in the church was located in the basement. But even when I drove there, I couldn't find him. I looked around and didn't see him anywhere. I called again and got no answer. At that point, I began to worry. Where was he and why was he not answering the phone? Finally, after what seemed like an eternity, he called. He proceeded to tell me that the police had stopped him while he was walking home from work and that he had been unable to call me. Supposedly, he had been stopped because he fit the description of a black male wearing a black jacket they had been looking for. They had held him for questioning and had taken his license to validate his story with the ladies from the church. Luckily, they were still there. Who knows what could have happened had they not been able to reach someone.

My son told me he was afraid. He told me in that moment, he remembered what I had taught him. He told me how he didn't make any abrupt moves and how he had answered the police politely with "yes sir" and "no sir." In that moment, I was relieved and afraid at the same time. Just weeks before, Trevaughn Martin had been killed, and my son was close to his age. My son was merely walking home and he had been questioned as to why he was walking. Was there a crime in walking home? We lived in an affluent area called Johns Creek at the time, and I never knew it was a crime to walk home. That incident made me want to hold on to my babies even more.

I have always been very protective of my children and would give my life to keep them safe from hurt and harm. I made many sacrifices to provide the life for them that I did not have and would do whatever it took to make that happen.

As a single mom, one regret I have was that I could not allow them to continue with sports after my ex left. Because I was by myself, I had to work to keep everything afloat. I could not do it all and wished I had help. Unfortunately, I did not, and they missed out on some activities they otherwise could have participated in had I had help.

School was a struggle too. My oldest had a nonchalant attitude about school, and I was just glad that he made it out of high school. I had to continuously ride him about turning in his work and doing the right thing which was extremely exhausting. My middle son traditionally did well in school but got a wild hair up his butt in ninth grade when he met this fast, little girl.

I was so frustrated with him. He ended up failing three classes that year because of that nonsense.

I was fortunate not to have any troubles with my baby girl with school. God must have known I needed a break and provided me a breath of fresh air when dealing with her. She has always done well in school and now that she is in high school, she is excelling even more. She never ceases to amaze me. She excels in all her classes with straight As, plays flag football, is in the Beta Club and loves playing the viola. Thank God for grace. He knew I needed it with her. All in all, I made it. I made it with the help of a wonderful support system of friends who I consider extended family.

I was fortunate enough to have girlfriends who loved me enough to love my children and help in the most trying of times for me. Now, I look back and realize that even though I was a single parent most of the time, God provided me with people who could help ease the load. I am thankful to everyone who picked one of my kids up from daycare, or dropped them off to a game or even helped with homework. It truly does take a village to raise kids.

I have talked to friends who have felt like single mothers, even though they had a spouse at home. I can see how one could feel that way, especially if they did not have support from their spouse. Just because one may provide financial support in the home does not necessarily equate to full support.

Household duties, like cooking, cleaning, carpools, sports, recitals, doctor's appointments and help with homework, can take a toll since there are only a certain number of hours in one day. No one ever said it would be easy, but as mothers, we are always expected to hold it together. We are not able to take a vacation from being a mother. Whether tired or sick, we always have to be on the job.

One thing I would stress is the fact that you must take care of yourself despite the load of the responsibility. You must be both physically, mentally and emotionally sound to find the strength to keep going. That means you have to take time out for yourself, even if that means getting up a little earlier or going to bed a little later. Just finding thirty extra minutes to take a hot bath, meditate, pray, walk or exercise will make a world of difference. Just that little bit of time carved out for yourself will help you take on the responsibilities of the day a bit better. With a clear mind, and less stress, it will help you not to take the stress out on your children. It is not their fault and it is your job to make them feel encouraged and safe like no one else can. I used to get lost in a book or go get my nails done when I could. Whatever it is that gives you peace, do that and do that just for you. Don't feel guilty about it either. If you are not in a good mental space, you can't be in a good mental space for your children.

I attended school at some point with all my children. One of the proudest moments in my life was when I walked across the stage to receive my master's degree with a 3.5 GPA while my children watched from the stands. I did it for them. They were my motivation. I knew that I wanted to achieve higher income to take care of us, and it was imperative that I finish my degree. The three of them were my biggest cheerleaders, and I was happy to make them proud.

I am happy to say that all my children are excelling in their own right. All of them are talented and gifted. All of them are well mannered, know God and stay out of trouble. I am truly blessed. I am blessed because things could have gone terribly wrong. I could be telling a totally different story with an outcome that could have gone wrong. However, I am not. I hear the statistics about children being raised in broken homes, but I am here to say that my children do not fit that mold.

My children have no other choice than to be successful, because they have a mother who is determined not to see them fail. One of my favorite scriptures is, "I can do all things through Christ who strengthens me," from Philippians 4:13. No matter what, I knew that I had to do what I had to do for my children. The sacrifices were worth it. If I had to do it all over again, I would. They are my life and I do all that I do for them.

If you are a single mother, I encourage you to hang in there and never give up. Know that God will place people around you to help you do whatever you need to do. You may be tired, and you may grow weary at times. Just know that the sacrifices that you make now, will pay off in the future. I had many sleepless nights and have cried many tears, but through faith and perseverance, I made it through and so will you.

MOMENTS OF REFLECTION

As a single mother, my biggest fear is…

_____

_____

_____

Even though I may be tired, what can I do special for myself to stay grounded?

_____

_____

_____

As a mother, what am I proud of most?

_____

_____

_____

I Can't Believe I'm Homeless

It was early Spring 2012. I had been advised to attend a NACA convention at the Georgia World Congress Center to see if they would be able to help me qualify for a house. I had heard good things about them and had personally known a few people who had been helped. The program provided those with existing loans with refinancing options and those who desired to purchase homes with the necessary tools needed to do so.

Around the same time, a realtor that used to get her hair done by one of my friends told me about another option. She told me that she had several clients who had used a hedge fund program, and that the program would not take as long of a process if I went with them.

Since I was eager to reestablish myself and get out of the apartment I was living in, I got the information from her and started the process.

Basically, I was informed to fill out my application and compile all the necessary documents like bank statements, business license and the contract to the house that I had selected.

I found the community, put down my earnest money and gave the hedge fund company a certified check for $3500. I was informed that the $3500 would cover the appraisal of the home and go towards home owner's insurance and any other miscellaneous fees.

At that point, everything seemed to be on the up and up. I had no reason to feel that the company was not legitimate. I was especially comfortable because my realtor was the one who had recommended the company and she claimed she knew of others who had used them. I trusted her to have my best interest at heart.

They broke ground on my home, began building and I was preparing to close within four months. I had timed it just right because I never wanted to move in the middle of the school year.

The kids and I were extremely excited. I was driving over to the house a few times per week taking pictures and imagining how great it was going to be to have a beautiful home again. Before the breakup with my ex-husband, we had lived in a house and when I lived in Virginia, I had a townhouse. Therefore, it was really important for me to get my kids back into a home with a yard to play in. I was on a mission. I wanted to do everything within my power to make it happen.

I had started the arduous process of packing. One never knows how much one has until it's time to pack. Between working, I tried to pack something each night to lessen the enormity of the task at hand, but it seemed like a never-ending process. Even though I had been doing a little each week, it seemed like more was spilling out of every crack in that apartment. How could this much stuff be packed in a little over 1300 square feet and a single-car garage?

Time drew near for me to close but as time passed, I realized that something just wasn't right. Every time the builder's realtor tried to set up closing or try to get in touch with my lenders, they either weren't available, or they kept making excuses as to why the closing had to be pushed back. At first, I wasn't worried because I knew that most closings didn't happen on time. But after the closing had been rescheduled 3 times, I grew very concerned.

Since I was living in an apartment, I had to put in my notice a minimum of 30 days in advance. And because I had lived there for about 15 months, they allowed me to extend the lease each time I asked, since I explained that I was building a home and waiting to close. That wasn't the major problem. What I found out next hit me like a freight train.

The realtor who was supposed to have my back totally let me down. She really was a deceitful liar. She was really just a lying fast talker who was responsible for essentially turning my life upside down. And the crazy thing is, I didn't see it coming at all. It all came out in the end that she actually didn't have any clients that had used the lender and not one had ever closed using them. How could she lie like that? Didn't she know that I had 3 children to take care of? She lied to my face week after week like everything was cool, knowing all along that she had lied. What I realized is, selfish people only think about themselves in the moment. She was going to go home to her big house whether I closed on my house or not. And honestly, she hadn't done much work because I found the house myself. She wasn't even there when I filled out the application. All she did was review it afterwards. The house was around 250k, so she stood to make a good bit of money in commission for doing nothing. After weeks of not closing and the stress of having to reschedule the closing, the final straw came when I had been contacted by the builder's realtor telling me that my realtor had asked for another extension. Unfortunately, she hadn't run that information by me. I had no idea she had asked and this time in particular, she really should have shared that pertinent information. Had I known that at the time, I possibly could have changed the outcome. Her failure to notify me about another extension and the mere introduction to the people in general changed the trajectory of my life at that very moment.

I remember the night so vividly. I was leaving choir rehearsal on a Thursday night at the time, and I remember getting the call from the builder's realtor. She proceeded to tell me that my realtor had asked for yet another extension. The funny thing was, I had no idea she had done so. The builder's realtor had become concerned, but she also started questioning the legitimacy of the company that was supposed to be funding me, so I could close on the house. I immediately called my realtor and asked her what was going on. She told me that she had forgotten to tell me that she asked for another extension. How in the world could she forget something as important as that? Didn't she know that I lived in an apartment and had put my notice in? Clearly, she wasn't that unintelligent. I explained as calmly as I could, standing in the parking lot of the Lord's house, about how much of a bind she had put me in. If I were unable to extend my lease again, I would have nowhere to go and ultimately, be deemed homeless. This couldn't be happening? How could she be so negligent?

That night, I tossed and turned. I couldn't sleep because the night before, I had been hit by yet another blow. It seemed like the longest night for me as time ticked in slow motion. I kept staring at the clock and as I would look at it, only mere minutes had passed instead of hours. The dreadful thought of not having a place to go crossed my mind, but I quickly tried to dismiss the thoughts. Slowly but surely, the thoughts crept back in, but I didn't want to let them consume me. Finally, the morning came and then I had to wait for the rental office to open. Six, seven, eight, then finally nine o'clock! Geesh, that was the longest night ever.

Never in a million years could I have imagined what would happen next. I found myself in a position I never knew could be possible for me to be in. I called my apartment office that morning to extend my lease once more and heard the dreadful words that I will never forget, "Your apartment has been pre-leased, and they are scheduled to move in next Friday. We need to take possession of the apartment within 48 hours to turn it around."

Oh my God, I thought to myself! I had nowhere to go. In that moment, I felt the biggest lump in my throat. I felt like I had been hit with a sledge hammer. Had I just heard what I thought I heard? Was this a dream? But, it wasn't a joke. I wasn't being pranked and it wasn't a dream. This time, I didn't have a contingency plan because I was so focused on my home. I didn't go in with the thought that anything like this could happen. I immediately had so many thoughts flash into my mind. What was I going to do? I couldn't stay at the apartment, I didn't have family in the whole state and I certainly wasn't in the position to put money down somewhere else until things worked out. I was scared. I felt helpless. In that moment, I somehow felt like it was my fault. I felt like a failure as a parent. How could this happen to me? How? I had done everything right on my side. After the sting of the blow wore off, I realized I had no time to waste. I had to act fast and devise a plan immediately!

Initially, I was afraid of the next steps to take, but then I became livid. As the provider for my family, it was my sole responsibility to cover my children. How would I explain to them that I didn't know where we would go? They were extremely excited about the house. We were so excited about it that we had been riding out to the house a couple times per week to watch it being built. But, the plan was of course to have a roof over our heads in the interim. What would I do now? How could my realtor drop the ball on me like this?

When I called her to address her negligence, I think what angered me the most was the fact that she was reluctant to take responsibility. She half apologized, but that didn't change the fact that within 2 days, I would have nowhere to go. Yes, I said 2 days. I tried to remain calm and take the most civil approach possible given the situation. However, I'm human and in that moment, had she been near me, I probably would have jumped on her and beat the crap out of her. I tried to remain calm as I expressed to her how she had dropped the ball, and she had the audacity to challenge my Christian values because I was upset. She told me that I was supposed to forgive her and not be angry and that I was supposed to just "let it go." She was so sorry, and I mean sorry. She was a sorry excuse for a human being because she really didn't have any remorse. Really? She had a roof over her head. She didn't have to worry about having somewhere to sleep. However, in 48 hours, I had no idea where I would be. And the biggest thing was that it wasn't just me. My children! What about them? It's easy to fend for yourself in a pinch. But to drag along kids is a whole new ballgame.

The 48-hour moving process was an utter nightmare. I was not even close to being ready because I hadn't finished the packing process and with an expedited moving date, I found myself under an insurmountable amount of pressure. I pride myself on being strong, but this ordeal had me feeling like I was going to have a nervous breakdown. I kept telling myself that everything was going to be okay. I had to try and laugh to keep from crying.

I have always been a planner. I would like to think that I have always had a contingency plan or a "what if" in place. This time, I was dangling. I was dangerously dangling in a place that produced a plethora of thoughts and emotions that were extremely difficult to compartmentalize. It was game on. I was in survival mode. I had no time to wallow in pity; I had to put my big girl panties on and make some moves.

I had to deal with the realtor later. Right then, I had to find somewhere to store my things, secure a moving company, find someone to help me move and finally find some temporary housing for my kids and me. All of that would have to be done in the next 48 hours!

That Saturday and Sunday, my oldest son and one of his friends began packing the things that I hadn't packed. I had called and scheduled a moving company as soon as I found out I had to move, and I had negotiated an hourly price. On Sunday, when the movers arrived, all hell broke loose. The movers went into the apartment and came out claiming I actually needed two trucks. I didn't mention the fact that they were already three hours late when they finally arrived. My back was up against the wall. It was too late to try to call another moving company, especially since it was Sunday.

The manager inflated the price of the hourly rate and basically told me to take it or leave it. I didn't know what to do. I almost lost it. I screamed in despair. If my son had not been there, I probably would have had a nervous breakdown. One of my friends from church came to my house and coaxed me to calm down. She rode with me down to a local gas station where I was able to secure a UHAUL truck. My plan was to let the movers move all the heaviest items for me. I was racing the clock before the storage facility closed to get them to put my items in there.

The movers put the items they had in my storage unit. I was not able to put the other items in the second storage unit until the next day. I was supposed to be out of my apartment, but there was no way I was going to be able to get everything out in time. It was virtually impossible. We didn't have enough man power. I went to my rental office the next morning and they told me that I could have one more day, but I had to move everything into the garage because the painters were coming the next morning.

Despite all of that going on, I was in the process of trying to become a master educator with my company. I had been up moving all night. I had called and left a message for my manager, but since I had not heard from her, I tried to drive in to work anyway. I was literally falling asleep on Peachtree Industrial. I had only had one hour of sleep the night before and my body was aching due to all the heavy lifting I had been doing the two previous days before. I was almost on 285 and she called me asking where I was. I told her, and she immediately told me to turn around and go home. I did turn around, but I had no home to go to.

Instead, my son and I stayed in Embassy Suites for the next two weeks. I had mastered how to use Priceline that summer. I was moving from hotel to hotel like a nomad that summer. I continued life despite the lack of my own bed to lie upon.

During that summer, I spent at least 10k staying in hotels while trying to see if I could close on my house. It never happened.

My other son and daughter were staying in Alabama with my first husband and his mom, and my older son stayed with me because he had a job at the time. My fortieth birthday came and went. I went to church and work like nothing had changed. I needed some form of normalcy for my children. If I was not going to be able to close on my home, I had to at least go back to the complex that I had been in before the move.

The problem was, there was nothing available. I had to at least get met kids back into the same schools they were in, and I was not going to give up until I figured it out. I kept checking to see if something came available. Finally! Finally, a unit opened up for me. However, when I went to inspect the apartment, I realized it was infested with roaches! I had never had bugs in any of my apartments, so I couldn't start then. I refused the apartment and my friend who was a maintenance man at the complex told me that there was another apartment that would be available. It was directly across from the one I had moved out of just months before! I had never been more excited to get an apartment in my life! I was just so happy to know that I would have a roof over my head again. I had to wait another five days to get into the apartment because they had to get it ready for move-in, but I was relieved just knowing I had somewhere to go.

That summer, I learned many lessons. I was grateful for the small things. Not having a place to live put things into perspective for me. I was blessed because I could at least go to a hotel during that time. It could have been worse. I could have been in a shelter or worse. That summer, I didn't miss a beat. I made more money in that three months' time than I had made at any time before. I was blessed beyond measure through my clients and my church. Money was flowing in and one of the things I hadn't done was stop paying my tithes. I believe God was faithful to me because I was faithful to him. I didn't give up hope. Even though I was homeless, I was always covered. My kids thought it was cool staying in the hotels. I was stressed about it and they looked at it like it was a vacation. Kids are so resilient.

They were my inspiration to keep keeping on. I could have lost it. I could have just given up, but I couldn't do it. My will and determination to not give up during that time kept me sane through the process. After speaking to my pastor, he assured me that I would be restored despite what had happened to me. After fifteen months, I was able to build and move into a brand-new house. That time, it went so smoothly, I could hardly believe it was true. I moved into my new home and still live there until this day.

I am thankful for the entire experience because it made me that much more grateful for what I had than ever before. Even though I had gone through that, I knew in my heart that things could have been worse, and I am humbled and thankful for the experience.

MOMENTS OF REFLECTION

How have you handled a difficult situation that you did not cause yourself?

_____

_____

_____

In hindsight, is there anything you could or would have done differently?

_____

_____

_____

What are you grateful for?

_____

_____

_____

The Unfulfilled Promise

We dated for years, on and off, and then we went to marriage counseling. During the counseling, things I'd never heard came out, and it was obvious that the actions were another stall tactic to avoid commitment. It had already been four years, and when the counselor asked when he planned to be ready to marry, he claimed he needed one to two more years. Both the counselor and I were surprised because surely, we thought that after counseling, we were headed to the altar. What I found was a man who was afraid of commitment, as he had proven time and time before, and it was up to me to set him free or to continue to play the inevitable waiting game. Though it hurt, I broke up with him and never saw him again.

When the signs present themselves, don't hang around thinking you can change the individual. When a man truly loves you, he won't have to continue to impress your friends by being disingenuous, saying to them, "I love her, I love her." His actions will tell the story. And basically, his words and actions weren't in sync. His mouth said one thing, but his actions were another.

Even after the breakup, his childish nature and immaturity began to rear its ugly head. But I knew that I had dodged a bullet, and it was eye-opening to say the least. I beat myself up over and over trying to understand how I hadn't seen the signs earlier. Sometimes, we can't see the forest for the trees because we've gotten too caught up and have hung on their every word that we've become blinded by the truth that is glaring in front of us.

Don't fret. Life feels like it's over, but it's not. The one thing I had to ask myself was, what was I supposed to learn from the situation? Did I cry? Of course. Was I angry? Of course. Did I feel like I had been played, bamboozled, deceived? Yes! Of course! But, as I cried and screamed and went through my plethora of emotions, I had to evaluate what I still had, though he was gone.

I put my big girl pants on, dried my eyes, and got myself together with a quickness! I had to look at myself and remind myself who I was! "I am the child of the Most High," I said to myself. That's his loss because my "Daddy" surely must have something better for me. Could I see it in the moment? No, I couldn't. But, I had to remember something that I had heard once before. The trials and tribulations you go through are there for you to learn a lesson, to make you stronger and finally to be a blessing for someone else. How can that be possible? Why do I have to have things happen to me to be a blessing to others? Well, it's simple. If I hadn't gone through the situation, I wouldn't be able to be here to share with you today and let you know that it's going to be alright, despite what it looks like right now. As I was going through it myself, you couldn't tell me that my world as I knew it wasn't over. I had loved this man for 14 years. Despite where I was in my life, I hadn't stopped loving him, and once we had landed back together that final time, I just knew it was for life. Isn't it funny how we try to plan it out and it doesn't work out that way? It's like everyone can see it but you, and when things dissolve and you're all wound up, you're now hearing that your friends and loved ones had doubts but didn't share them with you.

Amazing! Why didn't they say anything? Partly because you were so caught up and if they had, would it have mattered? No! The rose-colored shades were on, so you wouldn't have even cared to notice if they had.

It's a process. Letting go is a process and believe me, it's not easy. The advice from my counselor was to cut everything. Everything? Yes, everything! All social media, block the phone number--everything! It's hard but you have to do it, or you will continue to get sucked in to the cycle of non-commitment. In moments of weakness, you'll think that he'll change if you take him back because he's learned now. Girl, please! Run! Sliding in with great sex and broken promises gets old, and if you do, you only get caught up again in the same old cycle.

A little over a year later, I was fiddling around with my iPad trying to share something with one of my girlfriends. To my surprise, he was trying to FaceTime me, and I remember thinking how odd it was and totally random, to say the least. Since I knew I was over him by that time, I was curious as to what he had to say. I accepted the call and said hello. I had wondered how many times he had attempted to reach me, and I wasn't there to answer. He said that he would try from time to time to no avail. He explained that he had now understood what he had not before. He asked if we could get back together, and I confidently told him no. There had been so many times that we had gone back and forth, breaking up and getting back together, that it was no longer a desire. I had completely gotten over him at that point and nothing he could say could have made me change my mind. Besides, if I did take him back, where would we pick up? Would we start over, pick up where we had left off, or just jump in and drag along like we had don't in the past? I asked how he proposed that would work. Basically, he had embarrassed me in front of my pastor by acting immature and due to his level of no commitment, he had shown me that he'd never be ready to be a "man." I respectfully declined and felt great about it. I haven't seen him, nor have I spoken to him again. And it's the best thing that could have happened to me because I realized that God had something so much better for me in His plan.

I took a while to myself. After heartbreak and unfulfilled promises, it can be rather difficult to press forward to give your heart to someone new. Better yet, it's not fair to your new potential guy to pay for the sins and mistakes of the last. If you find yourself doing that, you need to check yourself and take time to truly heal from your leftover baggage. The new guy could potentially be "the one," but you will potentially miss out on that blessing if you cannot let go of the past. It's good to do some self-reflection to determine if your heart is even ready for something new. Everyone handles things differently. Some eagerly go on into the next situation with their heart on their sleeves and others take time for themselves to ensure the past situation is out of their system. If you feel that way, listen. There is nothing worse than jumping into something new with baggage from the past. Essentially, it's not fair to you or to the new person. Maybe you need to get out of your own way and let God take control. That's what I had to do to find "the one," and I'm so glad that I did.

MOMENTS OF REFLECTION

Have you experienced an unfulfilled promise?

_____

_____

_____

What lesson did you learn from it?

_____

_____

_____

How has the lesson helped you going forward?

_____

_____

_____

RANDOM NUGGETS

Finding Balance

Balance in one's life is essential to overall health and wellbeing. Not having balance can affect mental and physical health. It can cause unnecessary anxiety and stress, which can lead to more problems that could be detrimental. High blood pressure, aneurysms, migraines and insomnia are just a few conditions that can be caused from not having balance.

As women, we are known to be capable of multi-tasking, but sometimes, we take on too much and end up losing ourselves in the process. Sometimes, a simple "no" could be the difference between having a nervous breakdown or not.

I am often asked how I find balance. Sometimes, I have to allow myself to be somewhat selfish to do so. Many of my friends are just like me. They are hardworking, ambitious, successful, selfless mothers, wives, executives, friends, girlfriends, caregivers, entrepreneurs, coaches and overall superwomen! Basically, they do it all and sometimes that is the problem. Unfortunately, in some cases, we have to do it all, but even in that, it is important to take time out for you.

We are so busy putting everything and everybody first that we don't make valuable time for one of the most important people in the equation: ourselves! I make it my job to check the women I know. These are the times to be your sister's keeper. If you see your girl going down and not taking care of herself, let her know about it. Remind her that it's necessary to do this. I especially share this information with my girls who are in relationships and for those who want one; they better look the part too. I do my very best to keep myself up. That means I make it a point to work out, do my hair, get my fingernails and toenails done year around—not just in the summer—go to the spa for facials, eyebrows, eyelashes and brows and oh, you can't forget the massages. Massages allow us to escape for at least an hour while relieving toxins and tension out of our systems at the same time. What could be better than that?

Ask yourself when the last time was you did any of the things I mentioned. I hear excuses all the time. "I'm too busy, I've got to take the kids here and there, I don't have a sitter, I don't have it in the budget!" The excuses go on and on and I have concluded that we make time for what we want to make time for. So, in essence, if you wanted to do anything that I mentioned, nothing or no one would stop you from doing it.

For my married ladies, it is essential to find balance. You're so busy being everything to everybody and if you are not careful, you can lose yourself in the process. You do have a big responsibility as mother and wife, but you have a tremendous responsibility to yourself. Stop for one moment. Close your eyes and picture your family's life without you. What would that look like? I'm sure at some point, they would pick up the pieces, but the point is, you are an intricate piece of the puzzle. Your guidance, strength, organization, and support, among many other things, are needed to keep your house the well-oiled machine that it is. But, the key is you must be balanced and focused to face all that you have to face on a daily basis.

Just because you have so many things to juggle does not mean you can stop being the one your husband met before the 3.5 kids, dog, cat and soccer mom duties. If you do, he's going to think he's been bamboozled with a bait-and-switch tactic. Remember, he fell in love with that spunky, sexy chick with the cute hairstyle, nice top, skinny jeans and heels. Now he's waking up and coming home to baggy sweats, an old, oversized tee shirt and an old plain Jane altogether. Now trust me. I know this goes both ways, but I want to focus on us right now. You've heard the saying before, "Keep it tight and right." Since our men are visual creatures, we had better do our best to do so. We can't get too comfortable. I know life happens, and you may have to switch things up a bit, but at least put forth some effort so he knows you care. Sometimes, it is easier said than done, but focusing on one to two things at a time instead of the whole list is a start.

My man and I talked about this in depth. Ladies! Men take notice of the things we do. As I said before, they are visual. You may not think they notice, but they do! My man told me that a woman who takes care of her feet, will take care of other things as well. Just because it's winter time doesn't mean you stop getting your feet done! When I get my feet done, it's not just for the polish color or design I decide to put on; it's for therapy. I stand quite a bit, so soaking my feet in a whirlpool of hot water and having my legs massaged is actually relaxing and soothes my tired legs and feet.

Have you noticed that when you do have yourself together and you are out for date night, how proud he is to have you on his arm? When you get a wealth of comments about your hair, nails, clothes or shoes, he's listening. He's listening and taking notice that people see what he sees and that they actually take notice too.

MOMENTS OF REFLECTION

What can I do to find balance?

_____

_____

_____

How am I ensuring that I am taking time for myself?

_____

_____

_____

What do I enjoy doing the most and how can I incorporate that into my life on a regular basis?

_____

_____

_____

Shhh Be Gone......

My Uncle Ronald Bailey is the funniest person you'll ever meet. And what makes him so funny is his innate ability to make you laugh during the most serious of times.

My siblings and I were dealing with a very serious situation. Our mom had gone on with the Lord, and we all were coming together to celebrate her life, yet there was one problem. My brother, who's five years younger than me, decided that he was going to bring his girlfriend with him. Now the back story on this girlfriend was that she was mouthy, ignorant, messy, insecure so on and so forth... you get the picture. How many of you have had this type of person in your presence? If you could, you would just wring their neck, right?

Anyway, she was always talking, always running her mouth, always negative, making her demands and such. It got so bad that she had actually alienated him from the family, including his own kids!

Well my uncle knew about it, and due to the sensitivity of the situation, he called us all together for a pep talk. The pep talk was between he, my baby sister, my youngest brother and me. He pulled us together and said, "Hey, I heard this old lady say this and I am going to tell you this." We were like, what is he going to tell us now? He said, "Now don't you let this heifer come in here and get you all upset." He said, "As soon as she might say something, don't you say anything. That's when you get out your spray." We were like "spray?" He said yes! "That's when you get out your spray! We call it the Boo-be-gone spray! And every time she opens her mouth or says something negative or crazy, just spray!"

You may have someone come up to you and try to kill your dream. When they do, you say, "Shhh, be gone. It'll never work, Shhh be gone." You can't do it because you don't have the money. *Shhh be gone!* You don't have the experience. *Shhh be gone!* You failed the last time, why are you going to try again? *Shhh be gone.* You don't have enough education to get that business off the ground. *Shhh be gone!!!*

Do you know how many times I could have given up had I listened to people? People will try their best to stop the manifestation of purpose in your life. Mine started as a little girl, and I still deal with it today! Just earlier this week, I had to deal with some foolishness!

I was bullied as a young girl. Either I was dealing with it physically or emotionally. I was a latch-key kid, and I would go home and be scared to get off the bus because the girls who didn't even belong on my bus or they weren't supposed to get off at my stop would.

I would run and try my best to get that key in the door just as fast as my little legs could carry me. I'd almost lost the keys in my hand trying to get it in the door. Sometimes, I'd make it and sometimes I didn't. Moving on to high school, I was very active in the church. It's like when the enemy knows you have a calling on your life, he wants to do his best to destroy it. Sometimes, I'd get teased because I was the girl who dressed up with my Jean Nicole 3-piece sets and they called me "the church girl." I was really active in the church back then, and I was like wow, they want to talk about me because I go to church? The other thing was my knock knees.

What do you know, God sent me my dream man who loves me, knock knees and all!

Moving on into adulthood, it didn't stop. I was just minding my own business, but every time I'd turn around, there were the naysayers, always running their mouths telling me what I couldn't do.

I was setting goals even then. And those who really know me can vouch for what I'm about to say. When I open my mouth and say that I'm going to do something, or accomplish something, I do it. I work hard at it, and I do it. I write it down, I put it on my vision board, I share with just a few I trust. See, that's another thing. You've got to be careful who you share it with. You got to protect it sometimes. Are you a mother? If so, what did you do when you were pregnant and preparing for your baby?

That's right! We had to nurture and take care of ourselves to make sure that when it was time to birth the baby, it was at the right time. Otherwise, it could be involuntary and prematurely aborted because we were moving too fast or doing too much.

When I wanted to open my first shop, I had support, yet I had naysayers.

When I wanted to move to Atlanta. I had support, yet I had naysayers.

When I took on a new position. I had support, yet I had naysayers.

All those negative thoughts, negative people, and negative energy can throw you off of your path if you let it.

Every time anything opposite of what you know God told you to do comes around, just say, "Shhh be gone!" Say it with me! *Shhh be gone.* Get out your spray, and spray them right in the face like the pesky knots they are.

Below are some of the things that someone may say. After every one of them, shout "SHHH BE GONE!"

Girl, you'll never get that dream job.

You'll never find a husband.

You've been divorced; who's going to want you?

You're overweight, but you don't have time to work out.

You're nothing.

You're not qualified for the position because you don't have the experience.

Whatever has been holding you back, we are going to leave it right here, right now!

You can do anything you set your mind to do! Just do it!

DAILY AFFIRMATIONS

I am complete and whole.

I am beautiful just the way I am.

My past does not define me.

I am fierce and fabulous.

I can do anything I set my mind to do.

I am already equipped with everything I need to accomplish my tasks.

I am focused and driven.

I will not be swayed by the negative thoughts of myself or others.

I will let nothing nor anyone sway me from what I am supposed to accomplish.

I am the bomb.com!

I will not let my light be dimmed by anyone because I AM SHINY!

Don't Be a Bag Lady

In the nineties, there was a song by Erykah Badu called "Bag Lady." Some of her famous lyrics were *"Bag lady, you gon' hurt your back. Draggin' all them bags like that. I guess nobody ever told you all you must hold on to, issues, issues, issues."*

Excess baggage keeps you from moving forward. If you sat back and thought for about 3 minutes, what are some of the things holding you back from becoming the best you that you can possibly be? Could it be a failed marriage or relationship? How about things that happened to you during your childhood? Is it a past hurt from a friend or loved one? Maybe you didn't get that job you felt you deserved, and you haven't been able to move past the disappointment to see there was possibly something better for you. Whatever the situation was, it's time to let it go!

Have you ever had a conversation with someone and every time you talked to them, they brought up the same old stories? You try and try to listen, but sometimes, you've felt like you wanted to snap them out of it and tell them to wake up and move on. Oftentimes, you can't, especially when it's an elder or someone you respect dearly because you don't want to hurt their feelings. But, enough is enough. A little birdie recently told me that I have to protect what I listen to and expose myself to, and so should you. Time is so valuable. Time should not be a commodity; it is a necessity! We don't have time to entertain nonsense in this day and age. There is too much to do, and entertaining foolishness is not a part of your purpose. Ask yourself if what you are listening to is edifying you or depleting you of your energy. If it is depleting you, this person is carrying baggage and projecting their baggage onto you. What is the definition of edify? According to Merriam Webster, it is: to instruct and improve especially in moral and religious knowledge: UPLIFT; also: ENLIGHTEN, INFORM. Therefore, the next time someone comes at you with some of their baggage, stop and ask yourself two things; "Is this information meant to uplift and enlighten me, or am I feeling weighted and depleted?" If the answer is the latter, then you better run the opposite way next time. Shut it down! Let them know that at this point, positivity is the only option.

One would have to think: I have my own issues and situations to deal with on a daily basis. It's not a matter of being selfish. It's a matter of taking control of what is or is not beneficial for your future and your growth.

You may be that person who just wants to help everyone. You find yourself spending hours and hours on the phone with everyone else's problems, which leads to excess baggage. You go to bed heavy, you can't stop thinking about it and valuable time passes you by. One must ask, "Do I have the time to waste on this or not, and can I truly make a difference or not?"

I'm not telling you to be neglectful in all situations. What I am saying is to discern what things are beneficial to concern yourselves with. This type of behavior could actually be

detrimental to your health. It's okay to be concerned, but don't try to take on the baggage of others when you don't have to. Instead, help the individual identify times when they are unloading their old baggage on you. Sometimes, it's hard for people to see their own behavior because they are so consumed with themselves and their problems. If you've identified this before, consider a gentle reminder of the behavior and finally, if they can't stop, separating oneself may be the next option. It could be hard to do, but unfortunately, it is necessary for your own mental health.

Moments of Reflection

Let's do an exercise. Who constantly dumps their baggage on you? How does it make you feel? What steps have you taken to make them aware of their actions? Did it work, why or why not? Am I the carrier of baggage or do I find myself carrying others baggage. What takeaways did you gain from this exercise?

_____

_____

_____

_____

_____

_____

_____

_____

Write the Vision: Make It Plain

When was the last time you set down and wrote out a plan for your future? Perhaps you wander around haphazardly day by day, just seeing what life may bring. Do you have a 5-year goal? Do you even know where you'd like to be in 10 years? Some people don't know what they will be doing next week, or even worse, they don't know what they will be doing the next day. I call that "vision ADD," which is vision with attention deficient disorder. You don't know if you're coming or going and sooner or later, you're going to crash and burn. Over the last 3 years, I have made a vision board. Why? I like to hold myself accountable. If you can't be accountable to yourself, who else can you be accountable to?

What dreams do you have? What things do you aspire to do? When I was a young girl, I used to line all my dolls up and pretend to instruct them on various subjects. I was the teacher and they were my students. In addition to that, I loved acting in plays. I had impeccable memorization skills. I could recite a play from beginning to end with stage instructions included. I absolutely loved to read, and I was always fascinated in gaining more knowledge about various subjects. I excelled in school and was truly driven by the next challenge. The funny thing is, no one ever told me I had to get certain grades. I just equated success to As and Bs and would work my butt off to maintain the grades throughout my entire school career. Yes, I called it a career because maintaining a GPA is a full-time job.

I am mentioning all this because I'm trying to show that even as a child, I had a vision and I was focused. Throughout life's challenges, I still made sure to achieve the highest grades and position myself for the next chapter in my life.

As a child, something in me wanted to teach others. Those bears and dolls were my first captive audience, and in my mind, they were depending on me to teach them something important. Do you realize that everything you've done in your life positions you for your future in some form or fashion? Sitting back one day, I thought to my myself, "Wow Alicia, you were practicing how to be animated during webinars as a child when you were teaching the bears and dolls!" That's when it hit me! That's exactly what I do now! Everyone is not effective when teaching via satellite. It is not necessarily the easiest thing to do because oftentimes, the audience does not talk back. One has to create jokes and have an imagination to teach an hour class and not be able to see the people who are watching them through cyberspace. That was just one epiphany I had.

Then, when I was 13 years old, I started working at a local salon as a shampoo assistant. But, when I look back, I had a brush and comb in my hand since I was 2! I actually have pictures of myself standing on the couch in my grandmother's living room combing my grandfather's hair. Who knew? Who knew that the exposure then would have me where I am now?

I decided to attend cosmetology school while in high school. I already knew the earning potential, and I had a plan. My initial goal was to finish cosmetology school, attend college, service clients part-time while in college, graduate, teach and become a lawyer all while continuing to do hair and service clients on the side.

Well, I got a few things right, but not exactly in the same order, and that's okay. When setting goals and writing out vision, certain circumstances in life may take one off the path, but it is certain that with a little drive and perseverance, one can get back on track.

After high school, I did some additional night classes and worked under apprenticeship to get my last credit hours for cosmetology school. I was supposed to be admitted as an eleventh grader since it was a 2-year program; however, they let me in during my 12th grade year. I was determined to get it done one way or another. Upon graduation, I had those credits applied through the state and was admitted under the apprenticeship program to finish my credits. I finished my hours while working at Hair Essence Beauty Salon. I sat for my state board exam and passed with flying colors.

Let no one or nothing stop you from achieving your dreams and goals. Did I face obstacles? Did I have naysayers telling me that it wasn't the way I should go? Of course, I did! But, through it all, I was able to keep my eye on the prize. As a young child, I knew that teaching and hairstyling was in my future. I just didn't know to what degree.

Initially, when I finished cosmetology school, I had not started college. I was working in the salon and I was making great money for a 19-year-old. As a matter of fact, I was grossing a little over $1000 per week. My aunt on the other hand didn't necessarily look at being a hair stylist as a "real career." My fellow stylists out there can surely relate. I believe she felt it was like a hobby and honestly, I recall my profession being frowned upon many years ago. Supposedly, it was a fall back career when one couldn't do anything else, and she felt that I could do better. Even when it was time to take my state board exam, she was already enlisting a fallback plan if I didn't pass the test. Did she know who she was talking to? This was the niece who was an A, B honor student from elementary to high school who had graduated 14 of 267 students with an Advanced Studies Diploma! Why wouldn't I pass this? Really?

Remember the drive and focus I spoke about? Well, that made me want to prove even more that my career choice was just as worthy as any other.

Even my mother put her two cents in. She hooped and hollered about how she wanted me to be a lawyer, and she put down the fact that I was a hairstylist too. Notice how I said, "she wanted me to be a lawyer." Isn't it funny how our parents had the choice to define themselves and be and do what they wanted yet they project themselves on you to be what THEY want?

Well, we see how that worked out. I did exactly what I wanted to do and was focused and goal-oriented in the process. I did attend college and for my undergraduate degree, I majored in business administration with a concentration in finance. That degree gave me the knowledge needed to open my first hair salon in Hampton, VA. I went even further to obtain a master's degree in secondary education, concentrating in English.

Everything may not have fallen in exact order, but it fell in the order in which it was supposed to for my journey. There were some bumps, trials and hiccups throughout the journey, but that comes with life.

MOMENTS OF REFLECTION

What is it that you desire to do for your life but have not done?

_____

_____

_____

What are your goals or aspirations? What is holding you back from achieving your dreams?

_____

_____

_____

Write down your vision or goals and hold yourself accountable to achieving them one step at a time.

_____

_____

_____

About the Author

Alicia Y. Bailey is a global trainer, coach, author and speaker. With over 27 years as a licensed Master Cosmetologist and Instructor, she has encountered women from all walks of life and has shared many experiences with them. She holds a BSBA in Business Administration/Finance and MAED in Secondary Education. Born and raised in Virginia, Bailey now lives in Georgia. She is the proud mother of 4 beautiful children.

aliciaybailey.com
Also available as an ebook

Printed in the U.S.A.

Made in the USA
Columbia, SC
11 July 2021

41687330R00078